HOW TO BE A CONCEPT TRAINER

Copyright © 2017 by Tom Mitchell and
First Stone Publishing

First published in 2017 by First Stone Publishing,
an imprint of Westline Publishing Limited

The Old Hen House, St Martin's Farm, Zeals,
Warminster, BA12 6NZ, United Kingdom.

ISBN 9781910488478

All rights reserved. No part of this book may be
used or reproduced in any manner whatsoever,
including electronic media or photocopying,
without written permission from the publisher,
except in the case of brief quotations embodied
in critical reviews.

Cover and interior design: Stubbs Design

Printed by Printworks Global Ltd., London & Hong Kong

1 2 3 4 5 6 7 8 9 0

HOW TO BE A CONCEPT TRAINER

Shaping your dog's personality through games

Tom Mitchell
BSc BVSc MRCVS

CONTENTS

SECTION II: AROUSAL AND EMOTION

SECTION III: MOVEMENT

INTRODUCTION

When sitting down to write this book, I started off by thinking of every word and phrase that reflected the message I wanted to get across. I came up with words such as *potential, relationship, connection,* and sentiments such as *synergy between dog and owner* and *synergy between science and art*. Underlying these concepts was the idea that, when working with dogs, we should *inspire rather than deprive, promote rather than inhibit.*

When presented with a dog training struggle, a dog training challenge or problem behaviour, the fallback position is to punish or, at least, inhibit the unwanted behavior. Time and again, we feel we must manage the situation, usually by depriving the dog of some of his freedoms. But how would it be if we turned a negative into a positive and tried to innovate?

Innovation is a word used extensively in business, but it has a valid meaning in dog training. Take a look at the following definition:

"The actions required to create new ideas, processes or products which, when implemented, lead to positive effective change. While invention requires the creation of new ideas, processes or products, innovation moves one step further and requires implementation of the inventive act. Innovation also implies a value system which seeks to derive a positive outcome from the inventive act".

Marc Chason, Motorola Labs

Innovation in dog training is really exciting because it is only you that can be *your* dog's innovator. You can't Google and find a step-by-step solution to the challenge you are facing; every journey is different and you need to discover what works for you, and for your own, individual dog.

Dog training has changed dramatically over the past couple of decades, shifting from trainers inhibiting and punishing undesirable behaviours through the use of negative, aversive events to promoting desirable behaviour through the use of positive, appetitive events (such as food).

Here's the thing: not only is it possible to achieve the results you want with reward-based training, but it can also be achieved without depriving your dog of anything – without restricting his freedom, without losing his individuality, and without stopping him from being a dog. In fact, you can take his unique and special personality and enhance it further. This has equal application regardless of whether you are working with a dog who has struggles, such as reactivity in the environments he lives in, or behavioural problems or a top-flight sports dog.

With the increased awareness of training methods, there is a growing expectation of what can be achieved with our dogs. Getting awesome results from reward-based dog training, whether you want a biddable companion or super sports dog, is not simply a matter of handing out a piece of kibble when your dog does something good. There is a formula for success.

In this book, I will show you how innovative, reward-based dog training that inspires your dog rather than deprives him, will produce the results you want. We are looking for a shift from inhibiting behaviours to promoting new ways of doing things. But there is a further shift, which has greater significance; we are training *concepts* to our dogs rather than, simply, training behaviours.

WHAT IS CONCEPT TRAINING?

I have an all-consuming interest in dog personality and in my work as a trainer and behaviourist, I have tried to work out how a dog's individual personality influences training and, equally, how it influences the development of training and behavioural struggles. When faced with problematic behaviour owners often ask me: "Was it something I did, or was it always going to happen?" Of course, there is no easy or right answer to that question, but it helps if we try to understand what is going on in the individual by tuning into his own unique personality. The American Psychological Association gives the following definition of personality, which is a useful starting point:

"Personality refers to individual differences in characteristic patterns of thinking, feeling and behaving."

Personality is therefore hugely influential in the way our dogs learn in a training session, how they react to events in the environment, and can make or break their success as a companion dog or as a competitor.

The more I have thought about personality in dogs, the more it appears to me that it is made up of concepts. In terms of dog training, concepts are general principles that we want our dogs to understand in a lot of different situations. Some dogs have a natural propensity for a specific concept which others may lack. For example:

- A dog may be naturally more **optimistic**, i.e. he will presume something new or strange is good rather than bad.
- He may be more **flexible** in his learning so he can change the way he behaves or responds to a situation very readily.
- Some dogs are more **tolerant of frustration** when the outcome they expect – for example getting the toy in agility training – doesn't happen.
- Some are less susceptible to high excitement/arousal levels and have a **calmer** outlook.

These are just some of the concepts that make up the personality of a dog.

By looking at personality as a series of concepts, not only is it easier to characterise your dog's personality, but also

HOW CONCEPT TRAINING WORKS

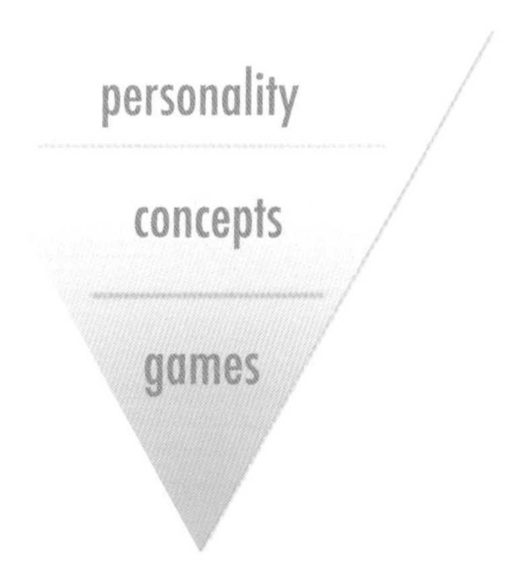

Your dog's personality can be viewed as a series of concepts which can be moulded by playing games.

FINDING THE RIGHT GAME

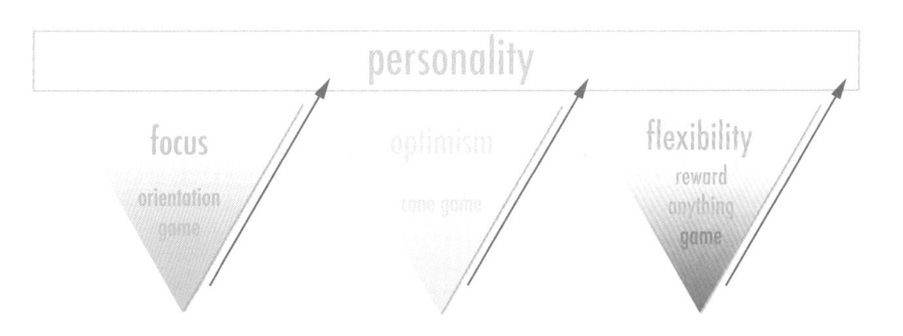

The skill is to invent games which will enhance a specific concept.

something really exciting becomes apparent. Personality is fluid and open to development, which means we can communicate and develop concepts in our dogs. By looking at it as the concepts with which a dog approaches a situation, and by observing his emotional responses and the choices he makes, we can develop some concepts to account for his weaknesses.

Concepts can be developed and promoted, and, in turn, you can arm your dog with the appropriate skill set to suit his job.

Throughout this book, I will be looking at some of the fundamental concepts required for companionship and sport, as well as some insights into skills that should be developed for reactive dogs. This is through a game-based approach – simple games you can play in your kitchen while the kettle boils, at training class, or when you are out on a walk. Using this method, you can teach concepts which, in turn, develop personality. This is such an amazing gift to give to your dog.

Every interaction with your dog has the potential to teach him useful and powerful concepts that enhance his personality and allow him to carry out his designated tasks – whether that is a recall in the park, behaving as a calm bombproof companion or competing as super sports dog – even easier.

Interactions should come in the form of awesome reinforcement strategy and super specific concept teaching through the use of games – and I'll show you how in this book. As you move to a training world that involves games, your training becomes a bit like a funnel. Every interaction and game contributes to a concept and, in turn, everything you pay into the funnel influences and enhances your dog's overall personality, outlook and decision-making.

COMPANIONSHIP AS A SPORT

In dog training circles, there is often a big gap between companion dog training and sports dog training. They are often looked at as entirely separate things, with some degree of snobbery regarding which is better. It is my strongly held

LEARNING FUNNEL

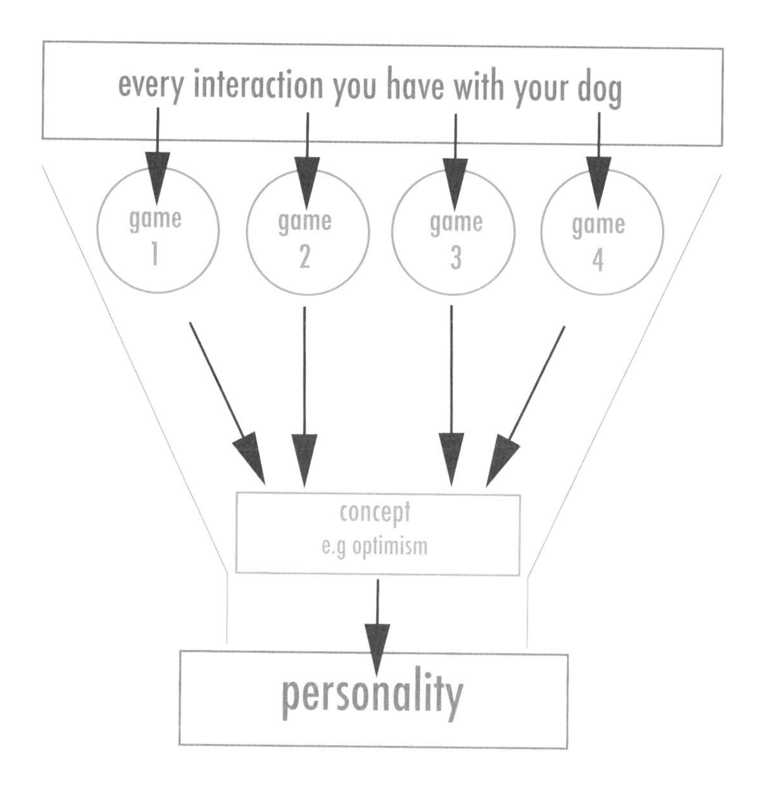

Do not under-estimate the power of interaction through games.

belief that the two are identical.

Firstly, let us look at the requirements of a sports dog. There are three intertwining components involved in sport:

1. **Learning:** A sports dog needs to learn behaviours, involving the specific criteria and the visual or auditory cues associated with the sport in question. This could be a retrieve to present in obedience, running contacts in agility, or catching the ball in flyball.

2. **High arousal:** A sports dog needs to be able to think and operate when he is highly aroused which might be triggered by the activity itself, from you, the trainer, or from a distracting competition environment.

3. **Movement:** A sports dog has to move efficiently and effectively; he may need to increase speed around an agility course or, alternatively, collect his body appropriately for heelwork. In both scenarios he needs to move in a manner that prevents long-term injury. Movement is a concept that I teach by itself, and will be discussed later (see page 195).

Now let's think about the components required for training a companion dog. Perhaps surprisingly, we have the three intertwining components of:

1. **Learning:** A companion dog requires a lot of learning to fit into our domestic lives.

2. **High arousal:** A companion dog needs to be able to learn and perform amid excitement and distraction.

3. **Movement:** A companion dog needs to move in an efficient way that avoids injury, just as sports dogs do. In my work as a vet, I see more injuries resulting from unskilled movement in companion dogs than injuries sustained by sports dogs – so this is a vital component for innovative reward-based companion dog training.

Take, for example, a recall in the park. The dog needs the **learning** associated with the recall cue, he needs to focus and perform this learned behaviour in an exciting environment when he is in a state of **high arousal**, and, finally, he needs efficient and effective **movement** so he doesn't run into the tree or trip over, which might cause injury. Companion dogs need and deserve these three components as much as sports dogs. Companionship is a sport in itself, and the only way to get the results that you want is to approach it in the same way as a sport.

KEY COMPONENTS FOR SPORTS DOGS

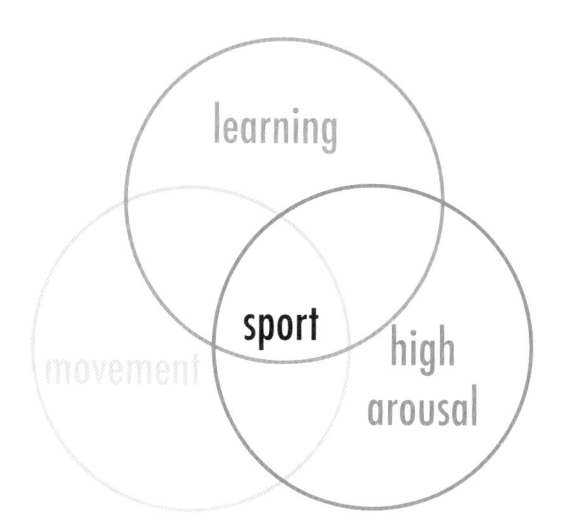

The ability to learn, to operate in an environment of high arousal, and to move efficiently are essential for performance dogs – and for companion dogs as well.

There is a common misconception that sports dogs differ from companion dogs because a sports dog must always be in a state of high arousal. This is not only purposeless but also detrimental; peak learning and performance cannot be achieved if your dog spends every second of every day in high excitement. Furthermore, it is important to bear in mind that every performance dog is a companion, to some extent, as well.

We aim for full potential in both companion dogs and sports dogs; innovative training allows all dogs to reach their full potential so they can be either a brilliant companion or a super sports dog. All of the learning, and each of the concepts, that are tackled and developed in this book are fundamental to both companion and sports dogs.

CHAPTER 1
THE TOOLS WE HAVE

I like to imagine a dog's mind as a big warren or network of subway tunnels – but not those used in agility!

These are tunnels representing neural connections in the dog's brain, and they connect various areas that involve thought and movement. Every time a dog performs an action, activity shoots from one area of thought to another by means of the tunnels, resulting in movement and the behaviour in question. These tunnels are comparable to the choices that a dog makes. So every time you put your dog in a new situation – whether it is in the park or on an agility course – he is presented with a number of tunnels to choose from.

The dog makes his choice, and this leads to an associated action. The action may be:

- Not moving.
- Going to greet a dog in the distance.
- Taking the jump to the left rather than the jump to the right.
- Jumping a contact.

Looking at a dog's available choices helps us, as trainers, to understand how we can affect, influence and change his behaviour – which is the cornerstone of dog training. If you envisage your dog's brain as a network of tunnels, what choices do you have to trigger a change in his behaviour?

You could:

- Block off some tunnels or remove them from the picture.
- Make some tunnels more desirable choices.
- Make some tunnels less desirable choices.

These three options represent three dog training principles: **management**, **reinforcement**, and **punishment**, which I will discuss in turn.

1. MANAGEMENT

Management is the process by which we limit the choices a dog can make, and remove choices that we don't want him to make. This typically involves limiting access to "naughty things". For example:

- Not allowing a dog with a poor recall to go off the lead in the park.
- Pushing food to the back of the kitchen counter to prevent stealing.
- Putting a dog in his crate at mealtimes to prevent begging.
- Using a head collar/halter to exercise a dog that pulls on the lead.
- Keeping a dog on-lead so he can't jump up when guests arrive.

Management stops your dog from making bad choices. It is very successful in doing just that – the possibility of choosing the behaviour you don't want simply disappears. It does this in the short-term, and will work so long as the management protocol is in place (no dogs allowed in kitchen, using a crate, head collar, etc.). However, as soon as you stop management, the tunnel reappears as an option and the likelihood of the wrong choice being made returns.

Does that mean that management is pointless and should not be used in dog training? Well, there are a number of very important uses of management and it's something that I employ in a variety of situations. Management stops rehearsal. In other words, management stops a dog from practising the unwanted behaviour while you work on the preferred behaviour. Rehearsal is incredibly powerful. What a dog has always done in a situation, he will continue to do – unless we do something about it! It's the equivalent of habitually turning off the light switch as you leave a room – regardless of whether there is somebody else still in the room.

Observe your dog and note the products of rehearsal; for example the dog that always jumps up on the kitchen counter as soon as he enters the kitchen, and the dog that pulls on the lead as soon as he leaves the house. By limiting rehearsal of unwanted behaviours, we can effectively promote and develop a more appropriate behaviour, using techniques I will discuss later (see page 64).

Further to this, some activities are intrinsically enjoyable and rewarding, so allowing a dog to perform them perpetuates the cycle and increases the behaviour in the future. Such rewarding activities may be jumping up on the kitchen counter and finding food, negotiating agility equipment without direction, doing zoomies round a training class, pulling on the lead and being rewarded by greeting another dog, or finding an enticing smell!

Management, therefore, has a very important place in dog training. It limits rehearsal of unwanted behaviours and prevents the self-rewarding nature of some behaviours, whether that is because the behaviours are fun in themselves (e.g. running around like a crazy thing), or they lead to reward (e.g. jumping up on the kitchen counter and finding food).

However, management should not be viewed as a training replacement but rather as a training adjunct. Strictly speaking, you cannot have effective development of a good choice, behaviour or response without also managing (stopping) rehearsal and outcomes of the less wanted choices, behaviours or responses your dog could make in that same situation.

However, new learning is not necessarily taking place as a consequence of these measures. Management stops new learning taking place, and that works both ways: limiting the bad but also failing to create the good.

Managing Rehearsal

As discussed, rehearsal of undesired behaviours, such as pulling on the lead, not only maintains habit but allows the possibility of self-reinforcement in the environment. So in the case of training loose lead walking, how do you limit rehearsal when you need to continue walking your dog?

In this situation, you must make it clear to your dog that the pulling situation is different from the loose lead situation, so that rehearsal of pulling is not detrimental to your long-term success in training loose-lead walking.

To do this, try the following:

- Train loose lead games using a specific harness/head collar that is only used for training this behaviour.
- When you are not working on loose-lead walking but need to take your dog for a walk anyway, attach the lead to a different part of the harness, i.e. the back clip instead of the front clip.

Rehearsal is powerful, and this is a good thing as long as we take control of it. Dogs are smart and will take on board subtle differences. Use this to your advantage and employ the tools you have available – selecting a specific piece of equipment, or changing the way you use the equipment – so that you are in charge of the learning experience.

Utilising management strategies also facilitates something else I am very passionate about – it allows you to pick your battles. All too often, I find myself working on a behaviour case or coaching a sports partnership, and there is one small problem that is completely destroying the dog/owner relationship. This could be something as simple as a dog that has not been trained to stay still while he has his feet wiped, the dog that steals food from plates, a dog that pulls on the lead, or a dog that cannot be quiet around the competition environment. The owner may have no wish to teach an alternative to the unwanted behaviour because other elements of training are viewed as a priority. This might be working on reactivity issues (in a behaviour case), or focusing on consistent and speedy contact behaviour (in the case of sports training).

In these situations, it would be far more effective for the owner to pick a battle and employ management in that one small aspect of their daily or training lives, thus enriching and enhancing their relationship with their dog, and concentrating on what is a priority for the time being. The alternative is to employ training of appropriate behaviours in all situations – for example, loose-lead walking, silence around the competition environment – but this should never be at the expense of your relationship with your dog, and should never lead to frustration on your part.

If there is no time, choose bigger priorities and/or management techniques that are effective (for example, not bringing your dog into the competition environment until it is his turn), then opt for this unless you want to train an alternative! In recent years, there has been snobbery around managing behaviour and situations and, in terms of the training ideal, it is certainly ranks lower than training an alternative behaviour/response. But if you are not planning on training an alternative, don't have enough time or simply have bigger things to focus on, then don't let that snobbery influence your choices, force you to perpetuate the bad situation and, in turn, ruin your relationship with your dog.

Finally and probably the most important use of management is when it may be required in dangerous situations. Our number one priority is to keep our dogs happy, healthy and out of danger. Sometimes inappropriate behaviours are dangerous and management strategies should be employed until the appropriate behaviour is taught. In some cases, they should always be employed if there is a threat to safety, regardless of how well trained your dog may be. For example:

- Using a long line where a recall is 100 per cent necessary.
- Using a lead for walking – no matter how keen your dog is on proximity to you.
- Restricting your dog before opening external doors.
- Keeping your dog away from medications.

2. REINFORCEMENT

We are all familiar with the concept of rewarding our dogs. By rewarding your dog for doing something you want him to do, you are reinforcing it – making it more likely that he will repeat the behaviour on future occasions. Looking at this within the context of the dog's brain and the network of tunnels, which represent the choices he makes, you are strengthening and reinforcing the walls of the tunnel he chooses. He is therefore more likely to make this choice in the future. As the walls become stronger, so the pathways in his brain are reinforced, and selection becomes automatic.

These new, improved, better tunnels quickly become the better option. If you were faced with a decision, for example, of taking a subway that was small, dirty, dark and noisy or the one that was large, beautifully lit and clean, with marble floors and champagne on arrival – which would you choose? Clearly a no-brainer, and so it is with a dog that is being positively reinforced.

Reinforcement can occur by two processes which are known as positive and negative reinforcement. The result on the behaviour itself is, by definition, the same – they both increase the likelihood of the behaviour re-occurring in the future. However, the application of the two processes is very different.

Positive Reinforcement

Positive reinforcement involves adding something good to the situation in response to the behaviour you want to reinforce. For example, you reward your dog by giving him a tasty treat or maybe a game with his favourite toy. This process enhances the tunnel by the mechanism we discussed above, adding in desirable furnishings, lighting and central heating/air conditioning.

An important note to prepare for later; it is not the food or the toy that is reinforcing the behaviour. It is the behaviour of eating or the behaviour of playing that is desirable and therefore reinforces the previous 'wanted' behaviour.

Negative Reinforcement

Negative reinforcement involves taking something bad out of the situation in response to the behaviour you want to reinforce. For example, the dog no longer has to endure an ear pinch once he is in the sit position (hence rewarding the sit behaviour). This process enhances the tunnel by taking something unwanted/undesirable out of the tunnel. For example, getting rid of the spiked flooring, removing the intimidating man at the entrance of the tunnel or silencing the harsh, and extremely loud, heavy metal music that is playing.

The issue with this is that the dog trainer must apply these undesirable and negative things in the first place in order that they can then be removed as a 'reward'. This process of learning goes hand in hand with positive punishment (see below).

3. PUNISHMENT

Punishment is the opposite of reinforcement. It involves decreasing the frequency of a behaviour and can be likened to downgrading the tunnel concerned. Again, it comes in two distinct flavours: positive punishment and negative punishment.

Positive Punishment

This involves adding something bad/undesirable to the

situation, for example a check of the choke chain or a pinch of the ear. This aligns with negative reinforcement, i.e. removing something undesirable from a situation as a reward. This type of training is positioning the intimidating man at the entrance of the tunnel, installing the spiked flooring and switching on the loud heavy metal CD, which will make that tunnel pretty undesirable in the future.

Negative Punishment

This has the same outcome as positive punishment, but does so by taking away something good from the tunnel. Maybe the lights have gone out in the tunnel, or the champagne is no longer on offer, making the tunnel less likely to be used in the future. In dog training terms, this is the equivalent of withholding the treat when the incorrect behaviour is offered or not allowing access to greeting a family member until barking stops.

HOW DOGS LEARN

	adding something to the situation	taking something away from the situation
reinforcement (increasing behaviour in the future)	positive reinforcement	negative reinforcement
punishment (decreasing behaviour in the future)	positive punishment	negative punishment

In terms of training, reinforcement and punishment are diametric opposites.

LEARNING HAPPENS

Now, this is important: learning *happens*. Learning happens whether we step in and direct it or not; this is how many unwanted behaviours can develop in the sports and in the companion dog.

Think about it; your dog progresses through the day from behaviour to behaviour and some behaviours are, obviously, more reinforcing than others. For example, the behaviour of running through an agility tunnel is far more reinforcing than doing a stopped contact without the right training. If any behaviour is followed by a more reinforcing behaviour, it gets reinforced. This is a big concept and underlies everything we do in dog training.

To use an agility start-line as an example: your dog breaks his start-line wait and takes the first jump. Jumping is more desirable than sitting stationary, right? So what has been reinforced? The 'breaking the start-line uncued' tunnel just got marble flooring, champagne on arrival and air conditioning. I think we can all own up to the times we have allowed this to happen in training.

Let's look at an example in a domestic setting. You take your dog to the park and then give his recall cue, knowing you are in a situation where your dog only responds with the appropriate behaviour 20 per cent of the time. Unfortunately this occasion falls into the 80 per cent bracket; your dog ignores the cue and fails to perform the behaviour you want. His chosen behaviour is to head off in the other direction, intent on pursuing a particularly fascinating scent. The 'ignore (or sniff in response to) recall cue' tunnel has just been reinforced and grows once again in desirability compared to the recall tunnel. The next time you are in this situation, there may be only a 10 per cent chance of your dog responding to his recall cue.

The same discussion can be applied to an agility contact (whether stopped or running) with the likelihood of performance decreasing with every reinforcing consequence of those dreaded optional tunnels, e.g. jump the contact completely, jump off the side, eye stalk, and so on… Dogs are creative, and life is very effective at presenting supercharged reinforcement – and not always of the behaviours we want!

CHOICES, CHOICES, CHOICES!

As discussed, it is helpful to look at each choice your dog makes as a tunnel, and the means of reinforcing that choice as upgrading the tunnel with, for example, a variety of soft furnishings to make it more desirable. In terms of dog training, this is our means of increasing the 'right' choices, i.e. the behaviour we want in the future.

WHICH TUNNEL?

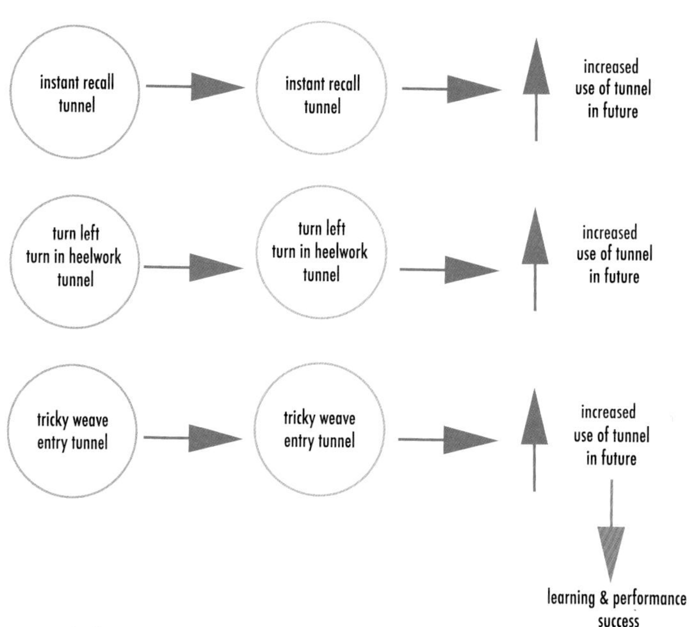

If a tunnel/choice is positively reinforced, it becomes the most attractive option and will therefore be chosen on future occasions.

This is seriously exciting because our dogs make a vast number of choices every second of every day. In fact they have so many choices to work through, we tend to take many of them for granted. But if you consider the decisions that your dog has to make on a second-by-second basis, you will start to appreciate the extent of his 'good' behaviour. Even the naughtiest dog chooses the behaviour we consider desirable more often than not, which, perhaps surprisingly, gives plenty of scope for reinforcement. This is the first step in achieving the utmost in learning, in performance, and in the relationship you share with your dog.

To understand this concept, let's think about what is involved in asking a dog to sit and maintain it, and what choices are available to him. When he hears the verbal cue/hand signal, he will work through some or all of the following choices:

- Do I head off forwards?
- Do I head to the left?
- To the right?
- How about behind me?
- Maybe I'll add a bark?
- A sit pretty?
- Maybe I'll relax my hips and let my knees droop?
- Maybe I'll tuck a leg underneath me?
- Shall I lie down?
- Or do I maintain the sit and wait for a release cue? (which might be the one you want!)

As you can imagine, there are even more choices than those listed above – and these are presented to a dog every second that he is in that situation; he has to re-evaluate continually. I like to visualise this using a choice funnel. The choice funnel shows the number of choices presented to a dog

NUMBER OF CHOICES

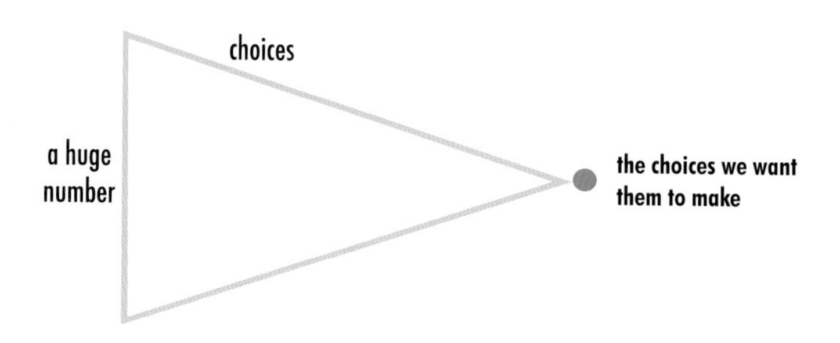

Your dog will be faced with many choices every time he makes a decision.

and how he has to work through them to reach the choice the trainer wants.

Just imagine the number of choices involved in hitting a contact or negotiating the weaves. A dog has to work through all these choices, dismissing them one after another, until he arrives at the choice we want. This gives us a real appreciation for dogs who make the 'correct' choices time and time again. Dogs are amazing, and training makes this whole process easier for them.

As we reinforce the choices we want, thus reinforcing the appropriate tunnels, the choices our dogs have to work through are fewer and fewer. It gets easier! As we reinforce the right choices and enhance the tunnel that is the single choice we want, the choice funnel becomes smaller and smaller. In other words, some choices become obviously incorrect, and the 'right' choices become more obvious.

Every time you reinforce your dog in a particular situation – for example, you reinforce him for not chasing a squirrel by tossing a piece of food in the opposite direction – you reinforce and equip that tunnel so it is more likely to be chosen in the future. On the next occasion this situation presents itself, there

MAKING THE CHOICE

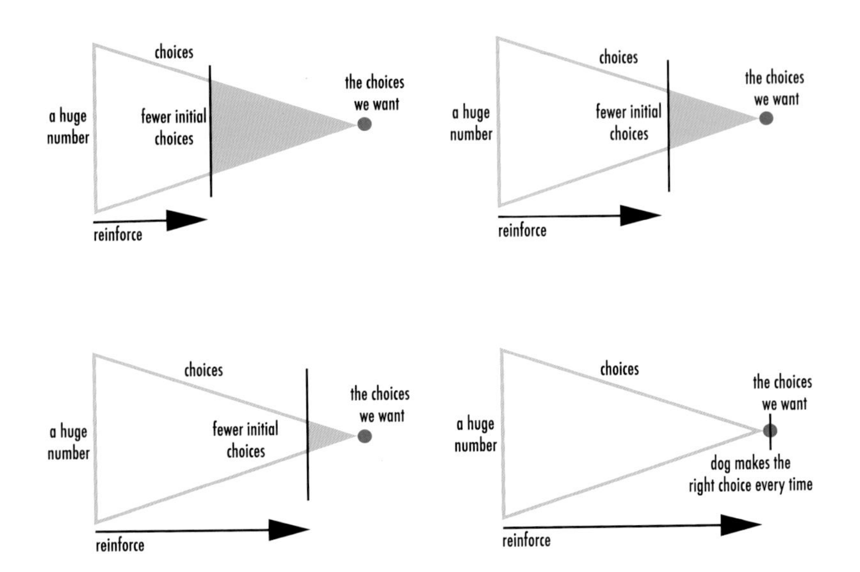

We need to reinforce the behaviour we want so that the 'right' choice – the behaviour we want – becomes the only viable option.

is now a more appealing tunnel – a more obvious choice – and that is the choice not to chase the squirrel. This is a simplified example, and we'll cover the way in which we reinforce to make this reality, later on.

Over repeated times where you reward your dog at a distance for not chasing the squirrel (never mind asking for an active behaviour, but rather the absence of an undesirable behaviour), the choice you want becomes increasingly likely until eventually there is only one choice that your dog even acknowledges.

The same can be applied to any choice, any tunnel, any dog, whether training for companionship or training for sport – and that is incredibly empowering to all of us who train our dogs.

A key element of innovative dog training that gets real-life results is ensuring that in all your cued behaviours – the correct choices are obvious to your dog. Equally, there must be no residual choices in the cued behaviour, i.e. no variation, whether it is a simple sit, a running contact or competition heelwork. A single choice that is obviously apparent to your dog, with no doubt over the other existing choices, results in a behaviour that has:

Consistency

Confidence

Speed

Precision

... and is a whole lot of fun and is rewarding in itself!

Achieving this high standard is vital for competitive sport, and for any behaviour where you want consistency. The following discussions will focus on how to achieve this finesse in all your trained behaviours.

TOP TIP!

A way to determine if your dog has this level of polish in a behaviour – i.e. no residual choices associated with the cue other than the one you want – is to film your dog performing the cued behaviour ten times in a row. Watch the footage back and note any changes in the behaviour; dogs that have remaining residual choices in the behaviour will show very slight differences every time they perform the behaviour. This can be especially telling if you repeat the exercise without rewarding the dog for each repetition.

It takes true understanding of the correct choice, and confidence in it, to repeat a behaviour in exactly the same way without any form of feedback from the trainer. For sports dogs, this level of polish is exactly what is required.

Management and Choice

As we have already discussed, management – the tool we can employ to limit choice/tunnel availability – has a specific role in dog training and living safely with dogs. A crucial application, in both performance and companionship, is the use of management in training a new behaviour and in developing and progressing behaviours. This is key to establishing those shiny, consistent, fast, happy behaviours that we so need.

Management can be used to reduce the number of choices available to your dog so that he is more likely to select the one you want. This gives you the opportunity to reinforce the right choice/tunnel – and then the magic can happen. Over time, you can wean your dog from the management tool and, because the tunnel is now packed with all the cool furniture, nice lighting and champagne on arrival, he will still make the right choice, despite things getting a whole lot harder!

Management tools come in a variety of forms depending on the behaviour you are training. For example, if you want to

MANAGING THE CHOICE

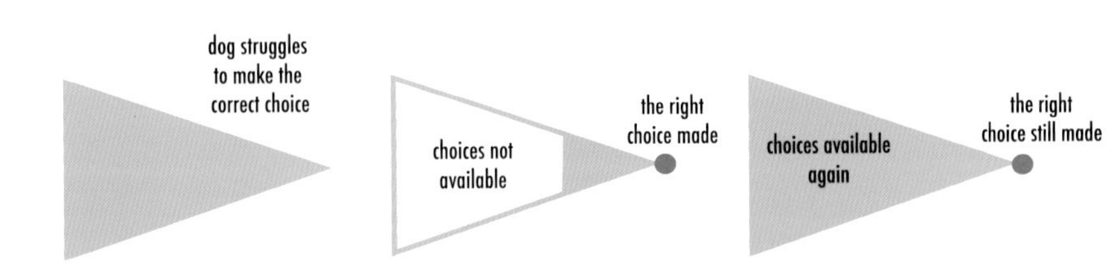

By reducing the choices available, you can help your dog to make the 'right' choice.

establish a consistent recall when you are walking your dog in the park you might:

- Reward him for offering proximity to you when on lead (or long-line) before removing the lead. The lead represents a management strategy of 'create distance between me and my owner' tunnel.
- Interesting objects or surfaces – this could be grass, for example, it your dog especially loves to sniff this type of surface – from the environment. Practise recalls and then re-introduce the objects/surface.

If you want to train your dog to place his back feet on a target, you might:

- Sit on the floor and place a cushion by your feet to limit sideways movement.
- Reward any weight shift backwards.
- Reward the moment one foot touches the target, and so on.
- Work on the behaviour in a low distraction environment before increasing distraction levels.

CHOICE-REWARD FRAMEWORK

If you look at dog training as choice rewarding rather than behaviour rewarding, you can take it to the next level. Why is this?

It is because choices are never completely specific to one situation, at one time, with no crossover to other situations. The choice that you want your dog to make in one situation might also apply to other situations, which gives you the opportunity to work on them.

For example, your dog might choose to:

- Target his foot on the bottom step of the stairs, rather than skip the last one (aka a running contact).
- Orient to you and run towards you (aka a recall).

- Stretch out (aka a bow).
- Stay close and offer eye contact (aka heel position).

...I could go on and on!

By reinforcing choices in a parallel situation, making them more likely to repeated in the future, you, as a trainer, are moving closer to getting what you want, where you want it.

The term for this is choice-reward framework, and it is exactly what it says on the tin: see a choice you like – reward it! The framework is all about catching those uncued moments where your dog chooses:

- To orient to you in the park (so rewarding trainer focus).
- To focus forward on a jump (so rewarding forward focus).
- To lie on a mat while you work with your other dog (so rewarding turn-taking).

The selection of these 'good' choices, which you can reward, may be in the exact situation you wanted them or they may be parallel to that situation. The significant point is that, either way, the tunnels are reinforced, strengthened and developed.

There are some issues that lend themselves to choice-reward framework. They include:

Impulse control

There are many opportunities in daily life where you can reward your dog's choice to exhibit impulse control. For example, you can reward him for:

- Choosing to wait for the release cue to go to a food bowl or to go through a door.
- Choosing not to steal the food from the counter.
- Choosing to walk past another dog without saying hello.

In turn, rewarding these choices works on:

- That super difficult weave entry.

- Choosing to ignore the squirrel that is running across the path.
- Choosing to take the A frame, on cue, that is right next to the tempting tunnel.

Running contacts

There are so many situations where your dog naturally foot targets objects. Never presume anything is accidental in a dog's behaviour – if it's there, it can be reinforced. Remember, your dog has picked that specific neural tunnel over the others he was presented with.

For example: does your dog target the bottom step of the staircase or choose to skip it? Understanding like this concept means the difference between progress and super progress!

Recalls

As you can imagine, recalls are full of choices. The best strategy is to break up the behaviour into smaller choices so you can reward them in daily life.

For example:

- Orientation to you: you could reinforce the choice to orient back to you (without cue) when it occurs naturally around the house.
- Offering eye contact: you could reinforce your dog for offering spontaneous eye contact while you are out on walks.
- Staying close: you could reward his choice to stay close.
- Driving to you from speed at a distance: you could reward those crazy moments of infatuation that happen throughout the day!

All these reinforcement opportunities are for choices that form part of the recall, and will serve to supercharge it. Understanding the choices that are presented to your dog, and enhancing them through reinforcement, is incredibly empowering to you as a dog trainer. It means you can work on pretty much any behaviour, any time, anywhere – and with zero equipment. All you have to do is break down the behaviour, think about the choices that you want your dog to make and then work on making these more appealing by kitting out the respective tunnels with the most luxurious furnishings, lighting, and climate control!

CHAPTER 2
ENTER THE REINFORCEMENT STRATEGY!

So far we have talked about how dogs learn and how, by viewing things from a different perspective, we can implement more effective and innovative training. This takes us a step closer to the ideal of achieving peak learning, optimum performance, and a perfect relationship regardless of whether your dog is a pet or a top-flight competitor.

As already highlighted, the key is to look at your dog's brain as a network of tunnels, each tunnel representing a choice that results in a particular behaviour. As far as you, the owner/handler, is concerned, some of the tunnels are desirable choices and others are not desirable. However, you can reinforce the tunnels you want so that they are more likely to be chosen in the future.

This all begs the question: how can we make sure that all the 'right' tunnels, that is the ones we want, are the most attractive?

It's all about the way we go about reinforcing these tunnels, the rewards we use, the placement and the way we apply them, and so much more. This forms a reinforcement strategy and is key to achieving optimum learning and performance. Flaws in reinforcement strategy can show up as:

- Poor understanding and learning in teaching a new behaviour.
- Inadequate speed and intensity.
- Inadequate calmness and precision.
- Degradation of the behaviour over time, for example:
  - creeping from intended location, e.g. less tight turns
  - creeping from mat/crate.
  - forging/lagging in heelwork
  - poorer form/shape to the behaviour, such as sloppy sits/downs
  - Reducing duration (e.g. stays, start lines).

When presented with dogs and trainers facing one of the above struggles, the solution is often found by changing reinforcement strategy. The key to formulating a reinforcement strategy is to match it to the desired, finished behaviour. For example, if you want a high speed and high arousal behaviour, this must be reflected in the reinforcement strategy. Alternatively, if you want to create a calm and precise behaviour, this, too, can be reflected in the reinforcement strategy you formulate.

Reinforcement strategy will put the power in your hands to select tunnels you want to be reinforced and ensure they are super desirable to your dog, and thus become an automatic choice. Whether you want a super solid recall, awesome running contacts, reliable weave entries, or a calm and non-reactive dog, the foundation and key to success is the reinforcement strategy formula.

When I am addressing trainers and behaviourists that attend my seminars and workshops, I make the point that dog training isn't all about reinforcing the dog; it's also about reinforcement for the trainer – and that only comes with dog training success. Tailoring a reinforcement strategy is one way of ensuring reinforcement for the trainer which, in turn, leads to reinforcement for the dog.

There are five elements which make up a complete reinforcement strategy, which I will look at in turn. They are:

1. **Markers**
2. **Reinforcers**
3. **Delivery**
4. **Schedules**
5. **Rate of reinforcement**

1. MARKERS

What is a marker? A marker is a word, action or sound that we use to mark the moment a good behaviour is performed. I prefer to look at it as marking the moment a *choice* is made. This helps you to get the mechanics of the process right and to be spot on with your timing. You give the marker when the right choice is made, and then follow with the reward, e.g. mark then throw food, mark then run with toy, mark then send to greet friend, and so on. The sequence of events goes like this:

MARKING THE RIGHT CHOICE

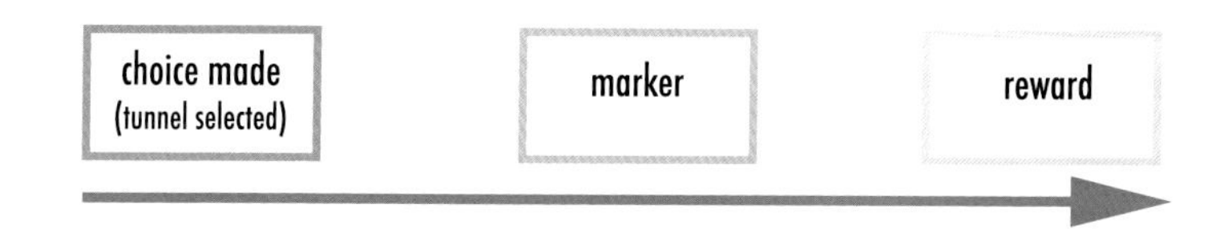

A marker will tell your dog he has made the correct choice – and he will be rewarded for it.

A marker that you will all be familiar with is, of course, the clicker. In fact, this is just the tip of the iceberg where markers are concerned. The clicker signals a correct choice, marks it and communicates a reward is on its way (as above). This means the marker becomes a predictor of reward for the dog. Because of this powerful pairing of the sound with the reward (click equals reward), there is value in hearing the sound, too. The clicker, effectively, becomes an additional reward in the sequence of events. This is a phenomenon that occurs with all markers.

However, that is not to say that the marker should ever become an independent reward in its own right without following up with a reward. The benefit of a marker is in the precise communication to the dog of a correct choice and the long-term aim of that choice (e.g. excitement, calmness, etc.) – and this goes beyond the value that becomes intrinsic to the marker.

Markers can include auditory stimuli (hearing event), visual stimuli (seeing event), tactile stimuli (touching event,) and even olfactory stimuli (smelling event). This means we can be creative with markers; there is a variety to choose from and we can use specific markers for specific purposes. So, when you are training, you can match the marker to the behaviour you are seeking to reinforce. In addition, the range of markers provides variety, which keeps things exciting and motivation high.

CHOOSING A MARKER

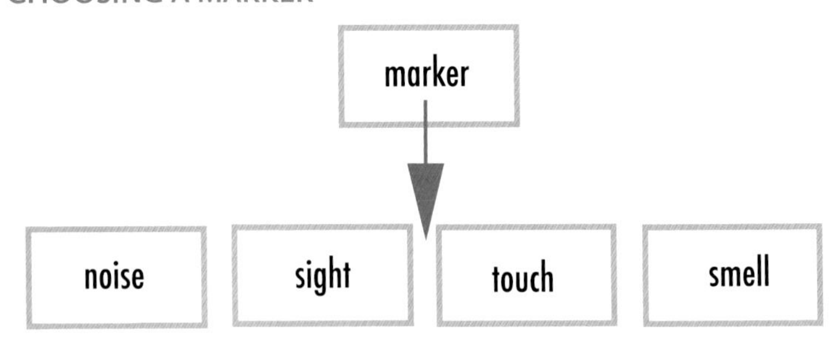

You can be creative with your choice of markers to add variety to your training.

Markers make training much more precise, bridging the gaps in communication between dog and trainer. They reduce frustration as you can more effectively signal the correct choice. You are helping your dog to work through the tunnel options, and select the most desirable, i.e. the choice you want him to make.

Further to this, each marker can have an intrinsic arousal level (excitement level) associated with it. This means some markers can be used to rev up a dog, while others will calm him down. A clear communication of the intended arousal level to associate with the behaviour long-term becomes part of the behaviour itself; you can decide the arousal level of the ultimate behaviour as you train it. This is a very powerful tool in working with dogs that lack motivation or, at the other extreme, those that suffer from over-arousal. It is also useful for dogs that need improvements in impulse control, precision and calmness.

For example, if you are working on a calm settle by your side, during your training class, you can utilise a calming marker which could be a calm stroke or a softly spoken word. This

MARKERS TO SUIT BEHAVIOURS

marker	**arousal level**	**distance**	**uses**
click	medium high	any	general high arousal training and learning
clap hands	high	any	marking fast and precise distance control in competitive obedience or a "middle" behaviour out and about on a walk
thumbs up	medium	long	marking a contact behaviour in agility or a distance "look at me" on a walk
"Yes!"	high	any	general higher arousal training and exciting skills
calm stroke	low	very close	marking heelwork in frantic dogs or dogs that forge ahead
fast-paced pats on the side	high	very close	marking a successful recall (the dog has to come close to get the marker and proceed to the reward - win, win!)

Choose a marker that suits the behaviour you want to reinforce.

not only reinforces the behaviour of calm settle but actually promotes it further, allowing us to reinforce again! This type of marker may be especially useful in those periods that follow an episode with a reactive, over-excited or over-aroused dog. In this scenario, marking that moment of pause and thought in the dog's behaviour, using a calming marker, will promote further thought and bring him back to a more suitable head space where he can make good choices.

At the opposite extreme, you may be seeking to motivate your dog to offer fast and accurate responses to known behaviours. For example, if you are working in obedience and you want a lightening fast change of position, you might utilise a super exciting, arousal-increasing verbal marker.

Further to this, markers can (often unintentionally) have an emotion associated with them. This occurs when the marker is repeatedly associated with a particular emotion and often happens when a trainer is experiencing frustration. Of course, you don't want any negative emotions to transfer to your dog or the behaviours you are working on.

Imagine marking your dog for doing a sit with a marker associated with a negative emotion (e.g. frustration) when you are in a challenging environment such as a town or a training class. Your dog could then transfer this negative association to aspects of the environment (such as people or dogs) and this could result in a serious behaviour struggle.

Alternatively, if a dog is worried in these environments, the use of the marker may trigger a fear response, creating a lunging, screaming mess before you know it.

TOP TIP!

If you are concerned that your dog may have developed a negative association, my advice is to retrain your markers, just in case. If you neglect to do this, the fallout could be huge. This is because the marker is such a useful tool – we use it all the time.

Sometimes your mood – irrelevant of the marker – may affect your dog's behaviour. It is inevitable that your dog will pick up on your moods, so the more independence you can bring to his emotional outlook, the more successful your dog training will be. This is particularly relevant in competition environments when you may be feeling nervous or self-conscious. One way to reduce emotional dependence is to develop a non-verbal marker, such as a whistle, a click or a tap, that ensures your dog is still rewarded for good behaviour on those days when you are maybe not feeling so reinforced yourself! Voice seems to be especially effective at communicating our mood to our dogs and, therefore, having a non-verbal marker in your toolkit can really help.

Finally, markers may relate to whether you want the behaviour at a distance from you or close to you. Markers can signal to the dog where the reward will be coming from – direct to him or from you. For example, when rewarding a stopped contact in agility you may want to reward ahead or on the contact, but you certainly do not want your marker to signal to your dog to come over to you for the reward. That would be a reinforcement strategy that failed to match the behaviour you want to create.

Equally, a great marker to reward proximity is the calm stroke on the side. I find this one useful for rewarding heelwork in dogs that forge ahead or dogs that tend to be very frantic in their heelwork rather than being controlled and accurate. As the stroke on the side (the marker) is dependent on the length of your arm, your dog cannot be marked if he is ahead of you. So, he learns to seek out the marker by staying in the perfect position for you to mark him. The stroke on the side tends to be a calming marker; it is ideal when working on those frantic individuals who do everything at full throttle, perfectly matching the behaviour you want in your reinforcement strategy.

Risk-taking and Forward-thinking

Dogs are very adept at pushing on reinforcement strategies. Your dog will seek out an opportunity, present it to you, anticipate the marker, and then actively take the reward. It is this process of forward thinking and risk taking that you need to take advantage of when training your dog.

Some dogs take such a positive role that you can find yourself being pushed along in the sequence; your dog starts to dictate the pace. This is not necessarily an issue, but can be counter-productive if you are trying to utilise a calming reinforcement strategy. Increasingly, you find yourself using reinforcement strategy choices, such as faster-paced, higher arousal marker, or rapid delivery of the reward (see page 45), that are contrary to your intentions.

The best way to overcome this is to film your sessions, as this pitfall is very apparent from an outside viewpoint but less so when in the moment. Remember, reinforcement for the dog is reinforcing for us, too, as we experience momentary success. It is, therefore, a very easy cycle to find yourself in.

Risk-taking and forward thinking are attributes that make dogs very trainable and, equally, can cause them to fall into the naughty but nice category. Your job as a trainer is to keep one step ahead!

Developing a Marker

We have now discussed what a marker is, how to use them, and their different purposes. But how do you develop a marker?

First you need to decide:

- What event do you plan to use as your marker – a word, a sound, a visual? This needs to remain consistent through development and use.
- What is the associated arousal level you choose for the marker you want to develop? You may want a calming marker or you we may want a high intensity, exciting marker.

Once you have decided on these two things, you are ready to create the marker.

Injecting the desired arousal level into the marker is achieved, in part, by the choice of the marker itself. Consider the difference a long drawn out "goooood" would have on your dog compared to a fast, snappy and excited "yes!". How would a calm stroke on the side compare with a more exciting, fast-paced buzzy pat!

The next step in creating a calm or exciting marker is by pairing it with either a calming outcome or an exciting outcome. The marker then acts as a predictor of something calm or something exciting, and will affect the dog's excitement levels accordingly. Remember, it is always marker followed by reward – and this is exactly how you train it.

Creating a perfect tailor-made reinforcement strategy for each behaviour and situation supercharges the reinforcement

FINE TUNING YOUR MARKER

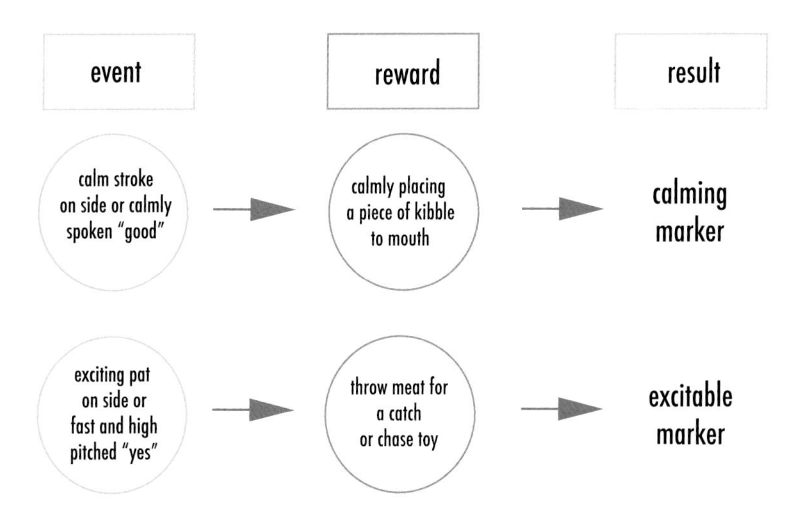

Make sure your words and actions – and the reward – are tailored to the behaviour you want from your dog.

of those tunnels or pathways and incorporates infinite variety Into your training as you create motivation, fun and success. I recommend you train at least three markers; in fact the more markers you have, the better – as long as they are successfully maintained. This will give you variety to work with in order to keep motivation high. But you also need to allow for flexibility in marker use for different situations – calmness, motivation, distraction – you name it, you can create it!

2. REINFORCERS

Now on to the second element of the reinforcement strategy – the reward/reinforce itself! Reinforcers are exactly what they say on the tin – they reinforce the behaviour when you add them to the picture. Your reinforcers are your tunnel enhancements; when you use them it's like going to the furniture store to kit out those tunnels and make them super desirable for the future.

In practice, in your training, the reinforcer could be your dog eating, playing, sniffing, chasing, or any other desirable activity. Take note, I do not refer to the reinforcers as food, toys, smells, or squirrels. These are, of course, rewards, but I find it more useful to look at reinforcers as behaviours rather than objects. This allows us maximise their use; we can also move away from always needing food to promote the 'right' choices.

The aim is to guide the choices you want your dog to make by way of reinforcing his everyday behaviour, whether that is sniffing, swimming, chasing or jumping. A reinforcer is an event that will increase the likelihood of a choice being made in the future as a direct result of making that choice. The reinforcer promotes the value of the tunnel that has been chosen.

The key to successful dog training, especially in sport, is to identify what behaviours are powerfully reinforcing for your dog. How can you do this? The answer is simple – observation! Dogs choose to do what is rewarding/reinforcing, so your dog will be telling you all the time what he most likes! He may sniff and hunt, eat, chase a squirrel, pick up leaves and throw them about, he may counter-surf or he may do zoomies. Presented with the opportunity, these are all behaviours that your dog may favour.

The powerful reinforcers for your dog are the behaviours you are prepared to put money on him doing. In a sports setting, he may gravitate towards certain pieces of agility equipment (tunnels, weaves, dog walk – I've seen them all!), or he may have his favourite behaviours in obedience (heel position, a sit from a down, etc.). When your dog shows you what he finds reinforcing, it is a brilliant opportunity to supercharge your training.

It really helps to imagine (theoretically) picking your dog up and placing him in different situations. This could be by the sea, in a park full of dogs, in a training class, in front of specific obstacles, in particular positions, in the presence of food or other animals. You then need to write down a list of behaviours your dog is highly likely to do without interference from you. Record these and build a database of situation-specific reinforcing behaviours for each dog that you work with. Then rate (or put a wager on) each behaviour in terms of how much money you would bet – £100 maximum – on them occurring in the situation in question. For example, it is a safe £100 bet that your dog will chase a squirrel when he is in the park? It is the £100 behaviours that are the most valuable and useful, so the aim is to get the behaviours you want into this £100 category.

PLACE YOUR BET!

situation	behaviour	bets
e.g by the sea	swimming	£95

Now, what follows is very important: reinforcers are meant to increase the frequency of that choice in the future. They are the tunnel enhancements that we have discussed, and your dog will continually give you clues as to what they are. These are behaviours that our dogs love. However, in many cases, they might not be behaviours that you consider desirable and therefore you do not want to reward them. Here's the thing: what we like and dislike doesn't really come into whether a behaviour makes a successful reinforce or not.

All too often, I am presented with cases where the behaviour the dog finds rewarding (e.g. eating) and how the handler wants to reward (e.g. a pat on the head) simply do not match. But, usually under pressure from an instructor or friends, the handler goes against head and heart and persists with the 'non-reward'. This is most commonly seen when a trainer is forcing a dog to tug and persisting with pressuring tugging of a toy when the dog is not finding that rewarding in the slightest.

This results in spiraling disappointment and frustration caused by the lack of results from training. If the trainer continues to take advice from people who don't know the dog, and don't see him on a daily basis, the cycle continues. I see this very commonly in agility training when a tug is used as a reward.

The best results in training companion and sports dogs come when the trainer:

- Identifies the personal reinforcers specific to that individual.
- Incorporates them into the reinforcement strategy.
- Creates new reinforcers by transferring the value from these naturally reinforcing behaviours (more on this later).

This gets the results that you dream of, and only when we do the above can our dogs reach their potential!

Further to this, within the range of behaviours that are reinforcing to your dog, some will be more reinforcing than others and have a higher value associated with them. What this value means is that the tunnel in your dog's brain, relating to that behaviour, has the most desirable enhancements. It is lighter, brighter, larger and therefore more likely to be chosen over other tunnels if the option arises.

So if you reinforce one behaviour with another, whether that is rewarding a sit with eating, rewarding heelwork with a chase, or rewarding a stopped contact with release to a toy, you are increasing the value associated with the choice that has been made, and the behaviour you like.

The value transfers: the fancy lighting in the tunnel you are using as a reward gets transferred to the tunnel you want to be chosen more in the future, or maybe the guy that is serving champagne is moved to the awesome running contacts tunnel... Taking low value behaviours that you want to build into higher value behaviours (in other words reinforcing them) is the basis of all dog training.

3. DELIVERY

This is the third element of the reinforcement strategy. Delivery is all about how you deliver, apply or facilitate your reinforcer, and I believe it is the maker or breaker of your reinforcement strategy.

DELIVERY FLOW

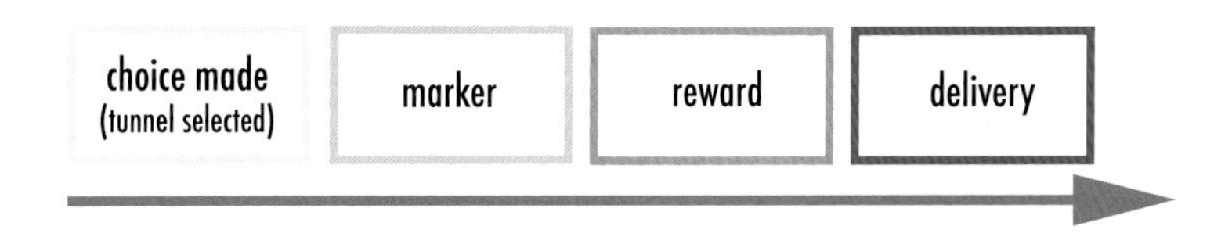

The correct choice sets off a chain of events which ends with the delivery of the reward.

Let's liken it to a shopping experience with a new dog food company. The website looks nice, the ingredients sound great, but the delivery guy arrived on Wednesday when you stayed in all day on Tuesday to receive it. What's more, when the food finally arrived, the delivery guy was rude, obnoxious and unapologetic. The new dog food company – in this case your reinforcer – may be awesome but you found the whole experience punishing, and so it had the opposite effect of what was intended! This shows how important reinforcer delivery can be.

Delivery of the reinforcer is dependent, in part, on the reinforcer itself. But it may include the following actions on your part:

- Throwing it low.
- Throwing it high.
- Placing it.
- Rolling it.
- Hiding it.
- Using the "Ok go" cue (see page 86).
- Racing your dog to the reinforcer.
- Animating it and incorporating a chase.

Each of these actions – and any others you can think of – involves a varying degree of energy in the way you facilitate the reinforcer. For example, you may place it calmly, or throw it energetically. In this way, you can use delivery to manipulate the degree of reinforcement, and to deliver a specific message to your dog.

So, if you want to reinforce a behaviour that involves speed and movement, you would use chase and catch in the delivery, thus matching arousal levels associated with the behaviour. The opportunities are limitless and allow you to choose a delivery that best suits the behaviour and associated arousal level you are seeking to reinforce. Before implementing different methods of delivery in training, experiment outside your training sessions. Your dog needs to get an idea of the fun that is involved in being given rewards in different ways. For me, this is of paramount importance. Developing reinforcers, and then teaching different deliveries for those reinforcers, is the first thing I do with every dog I train, regardless of whether it is a six-week-old puppy or an adult that has zero training history.

Reinforcers, Deliveries and Arousal

Reinforcer and delivery choice are vital ingredients when you want to build calmness (low arousal) into a behaviour or, alternatively, when you want to build intensity and excitement (high arousal). Going back to the visualisation of tunnels, I like to think of these choices as upgrading the furnishings and renovations to make them more desirable.

Building arousal and intensity into a behaviour may mean choosing play reinforcers and a delivery that reflects the aims, such as tugging, chasing or catching if you want to increase arousal. This reinforcement strategy would be the equivalent of fitting the tunnel in question with strobe lighting, a dance floor, a smoke machine and possibly a disc jockey!

In contrast, if you want to reinforce and develop calmness (low arousal), you would use a calming reinforcer, maybe food, and a calming delivery, e.g. slowly placing a treat on the ground. In terms of the tunnel, you would be fitting it out with sofas, classical music and mood lighting to make the choice more desirable.

Every time a tunnel is used, the associated arousal level is triggered; it becomes intrinsic to the behaviour.

REWARD AND AROUSAL LEVELS

arousal level:	low arousal/calm	high arousal/intense
Example reinforcement strategy choices:	Reinforcers: kibble, long-lasting chews, attention, etc. Delivery: Calm placement to mouth, on floor, cupping etc.	Reinforcers: toy, flirt pole, liver cake, etc. Delivery: throwing, catching, chase, tugging, rolling, etc.
Tunnel enhancements:	Comfy sofas, rugs, a warm fire, a harpist, etc.	Strobe lighting, smoke machine, disc jockey, light-up flooring, etc.

The reward you offer, and the way you deliver it, will have a big effect on your dog's level of arousal.

4. SCHEDULES

Following on from delivery, the scheduling of reinforcements (how often we reinforce each behaviour), is the next element in our reinforcement strategy.

I have found that this can become quite problematic as it seems to be detached from other aspects of dog training. However, I view it as a fundamental skill for all trainers which, when explained in practical terms, should be relatively easy to apply.

When you are teaching a new behaviour, you start on a continuous schedule of reinforcement – rewarding each time your dog carries out the behaviour. Once your dog knows the behaviour, you have a choice of four partial schedules of reinforcement, which means you do not reward the behaviour every time. This is done on a 'per behaviour' basis, so you treat each behaviour your dog knows as a separate entity with a specific reinforcement schedule that you have chosen.

Let's look at the four partial schedules in more detail:

I. Fixed Interval

This means rewarding your dog after a certain amount of time has elapsed. For example, you ask for repetitions of sit over a 20 second period, and only reward the sit at the end of this timescale.

This is the weakest schedule of reinforcement you could choose. It results in very low performance; the dog will decrease performance and slowly increase as the 20 second period elapses. This is not a rewarding schedule for dog or trainer – but we often fall into this trap unintentionally. The most common example is when you ask for a behaviour, and keep asking for it while you take seconds to get a treat from the treat pouch, and then deliver it. Anybody guilty of this? You may not have planned it, but you have put your dog on a fixed interval of reinforcement.

When a trainer has motivation issues with his dog, I often find that identifying the schedule of reinforcement that is being used, and improving it, is the key to future success – and all too often, it is the fixed interval schedule that is the culprit! This schedule is incredibly ineffective. As far as the dog is concerned, it is entirely predictable; it results in waxing and waning performance, and after the 20 seconds the sit may not be the best one with the right intensity.

II. Variable Interval

This is the same as a fixed interval schedule, but the interval varies. This results in a steady performance, with no fluctuations relating to time, as this is the element that constantly varies. So what is the problem with this?

This schedule still results in relatively low performance, and, if you fumble about in your treat pouch for varying times, you may be, unintentionally, employing a variable interval of reinforcement! Again, this schedule of reinforcement does not directly relate to the repetition of the behaviour itself, so you could be reinforcing the weakest repetitions.

III. Fixed Ratio

This schedule does not relate to time elapsed since a behaviour was last reinforced, but rather the number of behaviours the dog performs. For example, if you are using this schedule for sit, you may reward a sit every three times.

As you can probably guess, this schedule results in higher performance than the fixed interval or variable interval schedules as it relates directly to the dog performing the behaviour – not the amount of time elapsed. However, it does lead to a brief decrease in performance after the reinforcement due to the predictable number required before reinforcement. How can we make this more effective? This leads to the fourth and final schedule of reinforcement...

IV. Variable Ratio

This schedule is just like the fixed schedule, but the repetition of behaviours varies.

I work on the basis of an average, so, let's say a sit is on an average of three. Sometimes I reinforce after one performance, the next time after two, the next time after four, the next time after three, the next time after one, the next time after five, and so on.

By using this schedule to reinforce behaviours, you get stable performance at the top level. Not only this, you can select and reward behaviours that are especially intense or precise, or whatever criteria you are working on in your training.

So this is the schedule I use as the most effective component in my reinforcement strategy. The take-home message for this component is to create and build behaviours on a continuous schedule of reinforcement, and then move these on to a variable ratio of reinforcement to develop intensity, precision and even more value.

However, if you have any doubts at all about schedules of reinforcement, and specifically worries about moving your dog to a variable ratio of reinforcement, here are the two points that matter:

- Make sure you are not falling into the interval, time-dependent schedules – as we have seen, these are not effective.
- Don't be scared to stick to a continuous schedule if that is what you are comfortable with.

In terms of motivation, the only harm that can come from schedules is the accidental adoption of interval-type schedules. However, if you are on your guard and do not fall into this trap, being mindful of reinforcement schedules will give you interesting things to develop and focus on in your dog training.

5. RATE OF REINFORCEMENT

The final component of the reinforcement strategy formula is the rate of reinforcement, which differs from the schedule of reinforcement (see above). The rate refers to how much we apply the reinforcer for completion of a behaviour. So, for example, you give your dog five treats in swift succession and then move on. This would be more arousing than feeding him the treats slowly and calmly. You can also use rapid and slow rates to build duration into a behaviour by starting with a rapid fire rate when your dog is in the desired position, and gradually moving to slow, and then very slow fire.

PUTTING IT ALL TOGETHER

To recap, the components of our reinforcement strategy are:

1. **Markers**
2. **Reinforcers**
3. **Delivery**
4. **Schedules**
5. **Rate of reinforcement**

As discussed, you can manipulate these five elements to get exactly what you want – and now you have the understanding to adapt each one to your desired outcome, regardless of whether you are training a companion dog or a sports dog.

Consider teaching your dog to lie down, very quickly on cue, at a distance. You could utilise the following:

- **Marker:** A long-distance marker, such as a thumbs up.
- **Reinforcer:** A high value reinforcer, such as food or a toy.
- **Delivery:** Running to the dog or throwing the reward and long distance placement of the reward.
- **Schedule:** A continuous schedule of reinforcement while your dog is learning.
- **Rate of reinforcement:** Once you have the initial down at a distance, a single fire rate progressing to a rapid fire rate to develop duration in the behaviour.

Obviously, your choices for each component would be completely different if you were working on a calm settle to use when you are at a seminar, the vet's waiting room, or at a training class. In this situation you would use the following:

- **Marker:** Calm stroke on the side.
- **Reinforcer:** Kibble.
- **Delivery:** Brought directly to mouth.

- **Schedule:** A continuous schedule of reinforcement while your dog is learning.
- **Rate of reinforcement:** A steady but slow rate of reinforcement to build further calmness into the behaviour and ensure you are rewarding at points of true stillness and muscle relaxation.

Breaking down the reinforcement and adapting each component to your desired outcome gives rise to the process I call **shaping through reinforcement**. The nature of the reinforcement influences the next performance of the behaviour so that it can be reinforced again, and so on, and so on.

Reinforcement strategy influences and develops far more than the behaviour at that given time. It drives the behaviour in different directions, influences the associated arousal levels and even affects the emotional state that will be triggered when that behaviour is cued in the future. The great bonus is that the dog never gets it wrong. You work towards and achieve the behaviours you want through the very best in positive reinforcement – and you can apply it to any situation.

CHAPTER 3
TRAINING FOR FOCUS

Focus, by definition, means paying particular attention to something or someone. With reference to dog training, this does not necessarily mean focusing on you, the trainer. In competitive sports, such as agility and obedience, there will be times when you want your dog to focus independently, looking down a line of jumps, or fixing on a distant spot for a sendaway.

Focus should therefore be split into trainer focus and forward focus, and each makes up the series of behaviours that you want from your dog. For example, you want your dog to

TYPES OF FOCUS

trainer focus	forward focus
Eye contact to trainer Orientation to trainer No sniffing Proximity Offering focus behaviours as invitation to the trainer for work	Eye contact to obstacle, target, etc. Orientation away from trainer No sniffing

Depending on the behaviour you want, your dog will need to focus on you, or to focus ahead.

give you eye contact in heelwork, but you want him look at the first obstacle when he is in an agility start-line. The more you build value in these behaviours, the more you develop the skill of focus so that your dog chooses trainer focus or forward focus in place of distractions.

The concept of trainer focus and forward focus can be clarified if you look at them in terms of paying into bank accounts. For example, you give a reward for eye contact/orientiation, or you play a rewarding game that encourages forward focus. This not only rewards the specific behaviour, it puts more money in the focus bank account so it makes other choices easier. So, for example, your dog will choose to orientate away from a distraction so that he can focus on you. The specific behaviours that are being reinforced are not as important as the skill that is being developed in investing in the bank account.

There are many benefits to creating a focus framework whereby the default is trainer focus, and where forward focus is triggered in response to environmental or trainer cues, which could be agility equipment or a dead toy on the ground. It puts an end to 'eyeing' dogs, people, and other distractions which can provoke an unwanted response. When a dog knows he is being eyed, he may bark, lunge or even attack, and the dog that started the interaction may subsequently develop reactivity to other dogs himself. A focus framework helps prevent the development of leash reactivity and eliminates those occasions when your dog ignores you in favour of focusing on something in the environment.

If you make trainer focus the default, you are not sacrificing forward focus which you need in agility and many of the other competitive sports. In fact, you are making it stronger as now it becomes something special because it is reserved for specific forward focus opportunities.

By developing a focus framework, you make your dog's life so much easier. You build value in the pathways that *you* want so that his life is not full of second-by-second, ambiguous decisions, often allied with disappointment when he makes the wrong choice. Increasingly, the 'right' tunnels become more obvious to him. The results are tangible; as ambiguity and confusion decrease, speed, motivation, learning and consistency increase – and dog training is fun!

Focus also forms the foundation for impulse control. If you create high value for focus, your dog is more likely to choose this option – even when faced with big temptations such as pursuing the squirrel he has just spotted in the distance. The more you reinforce focus-associated behaviour pathways in your dog's brain, the more likely they will be chosen and, in turn, the more skilled your dog becomes at focus. This means that you don't have to work on every temptation your dog faces. As focus as a concept strengthens, he will increasingly make the right choice and he will apply this to new situations as they arise.

Focus plays an important role in preventing behavioural struggles relating to negative associations – for example, dog-dog reactivity. A focus framework will create a confident dog because:

- It reduces confusion/ambiguity, which increases confidence.
- It provides a high-value and appropriate coping strategy so a dog can deal with situations where he feels comfortable because he can focus on his owner.
- Puts an end to eyeing/staring, which can often provoke an unwanted response.
- Keeps your dog out of danger because he has an automatic re-engagement with you, rather than interacting with a potentially scary environment.

ENCOURAGING FOCUS

trainer focus	forward focus
eye contact	**1. Race to dead toy/food bowl** Throw a toy (or place a food bowl) ahead of your dog, restrain him and release him when he is looking at the object. To add intensity and value, race him to the object and try to get there before him!
orientation game	**2. The duration forward focus game** This is a race to dead toy/food bowl game that is for more experienced dogs with the game where they are held for a varying period maintaining eye contact on the object before being released. If you are finding your dog isn't able to focus forward for the duration you are asking, go back a few steps.
head off the floor game	**3. Whip-it games** Attaching a toy to the end of a horse lunge whip is a great way of building forward focus. Firstly, get your dog to chase the toy and focus on it completely. The rules of the game are that if the toy is still, then the dog should be still and focusing forward on to it. As soon as the toy moves, the dog can move! If your dog tries to grab the toy when it isn't in motion, then simply flip it out of the way and continue flipping it until he learns that stillness progresses the game. You can incorporate asking for cued behaviours with forward focus and reward with making the toy move and chase!
proximity	**Boundary Games**
4. Retrieve	

The game you play with your dog will depend on the type of focus you are seeking to encourage.

GAMES TO PLAY

There are a number of games you can play with your dog which encourage both trainer focus and independent forward focus.

Trainer Focus

Eye contact

- Sit in front of your dog with some of his dinner in your hand.
- Wait until he looks up at you and feed him a piece of his dinner.
- Build this game up, waiting until your dog makes direct eye contact before feeding him.
- You can progress this game by seeing if the dog can maintain eye contact while you move the food around in your hand. If he co-operates – feed!

Orientation game

This game builds a dog that wants to orient back to back to his handler, bounces away from distraction and loves to face you. Start the game in an easy, low distraction environment.

- Throw a piece of your dog's dinner out (to a distance of approximately one metre).
- When he has finished eating, he will look back at you, hoping for more food. At that moment of orienting back to you, mark the movement with a "yes" or a click.
- If your dog doesn't look back at you right away, just wait him out and mark the moment he does. Often, the longer the wait, the more powerful the learning – so don't be disheartened. You can also start this game on lead to encourage focus.
- Follow the marker "yes"/click marker with the reward of throwing another piece of food to continue the game.
- Play this game everywhere!

Head off the ground

This game is great for dogs that like to have their head to the ground sniffing and where scenting challenges their focus on you.

- To play the game, simply mark and reward your dog every time he lifts his head from the ground. The delivery of the reward is most effective directly to the mouth.
- Start this game at home but quickly take it on the road to environments where your dog may be more inclined to sniff.

Forward Focus

Race to dead toy/food bowl

- Throw a toy (or place a food bowl) ahead of your dog.
- Restrain him and only release him when he is looking at the object.
- To add intensity and value, race him to the toy/food bowl and try and get there first!

Duration forward focus

This is a race to a dead toy/food bowl game that is for more experienced dogs.

- For this game, the dog has to maintain eye contact on the object for varying periods before being released.
- If your dog fails to focus forward for the duration you are asking, go back a few steps.

Whip it!

Attaching a toy to the end of a horse lunge whip, or using a flirt pole, is a great way of building forward focus.

- First, get your dog to chase the toy and focus on it completely. The rules of the game are that if the toy is still, the dog should be still and focusing forward on to it.

As soon as the toy moves, the dog can move.

- If your dog tries to grab the toy when it isn't in motion, simply flip it out of the way and continue flipping it until he learns that stillness progresses the game. You can incorporate asking for cued behaviours with forward focus – e.g. a sit or a down – and reward with making the toy move.

Trainer Focus/Forward Focus

Retrieve

The retrieve to hand is a huge balancer of forward focus and trainer focus because the exercise is perfectly split between the two.

BUILDING FOCUS AS A CONCEPT

The key to building focus as a concept rather than a couple of isolated behaviours is simple – it has to be 24/7! A dog learns regardless of whether he is in a training session or not. It is therefore essential to develop this focus framework in a fluid and progressive way throughout each and every day.

How does this work? Well, let's say you see your dog give you a glance when you are outside in the garden or on a walk – you could then mark that behaviour and give an appropriate reinforcer. Equally, you could do this for orientation towards you.

This is an invaluable opportunity to capture those moments when your dog shows intense focus on you. For example, when you return from work or after a period of absence from home, your dog will show increased interest in you. You can use this to your advantage by marking and rewarding the behaviours that represent a focused dog.

There is another reason why you need to take a fluid and progressive approach to training a focus framework. Dogs need to generalise a learnt behaviour; the focus framework therefore needs to become part of everyday life, experienced in a wide variety of situations. If you build value for focus associated behaviours at different times and in different places, they will become components in your dog's thinking and will help him to make valid choices.

In addition, if you adopt a 24/7 dog training point of view, you can better transition your dog from cued focus, e.g. using his name or asking for specific behaviours, to default behaviours which are uncued, because you capture those moments when your dog offers them naturally.

By reinforcing focus-associated behaviours that are offered throughout the day you can:

- Capture moments of exuberant focus when they occur.
- Promote generalisation so your dog learns to focus everywhere and anywhere.
- Encourage better transition from cueing focus to offering of focus.

Equally in building forward focus, it's all about ensuring what you want and sticking to it 24/7. For example, if you want forward focus on an obstacle, target, dead toy or food bowl, then make sure you only send your dog when he is looking at it. If he is not looking at it, then wait him out!

"DO I NEED THAT?"

This is a concept that I find really useful in approaching any, and every, dog training struggle or goal. Simply ask yourself – "Do I need that?"

When you are training your dog, you may be encouraging or discouraging certain aspects of his behaviour simply by the way you are implementing the exercise, or by the way you are responding to him. Despite your best efforts, this can lead to negative fall-out in your training – and what is worse, you are not even aware of what is happening. By adopting the "Do I need that?" attitude, you will start to question what is going on and start to focus on what really matters.

On a weekly basis, I work with dogs who have significant and serious behaviour problems which, for a large part, stem from training where the "Do I need that?" attitude has been ignored.

No owner or handler intended to have a dog that:

- Is reactive to dogs/people/noises/etc.
- Knocks poles.
- Barks constantly.
- Nips his handler.
- Cannot be calm and settled in any, or all, environments.
- Does not perform to the best of his ability.
- Cannot exhibit impulse control.
- Is prone to injury.
- Will never reveal that secret level of learning and performance.

However, these things happen – even to the most conscientious dog trainer. Fortunately, they can be resolved and it is rewarding to work on the issue involved and see relationships blossom and success ensue. However, by adopting the "Do I need that?" attitude, you can nip these problems in the bud, removing any negative effects that result from your training. In the process, you will unlock the door to infinite dog training fun (for dog and trainer) and infinite relationship success! This is an exciting prospect – but what exactly is the "Do I need that?" attitude?

As we know already, there is more than one way to train a behaviour. The "Do I need that?" attitude makes us question whether we need to train certain things in certain ways, and whether we need to incorporate a particular emotion or arousal level into the finished behaviour. As a trainer, you begin to ask yourself whether there is a better a way; maybe it is something specific to the dog in front of you, the choices you wish to develop and promote, and those choices you wish to reduce.

Ask yourself the following:

- Do I need to use intimidation?
- Do I need to use positive punishment and negative reinforcement?
- Do I need to develop this level of frustration in my dog training?
- Do I need to pressure my dog so much?
- Do I need to signal incorrect behaviour to my dog (no reward markers)?
- Do I need my dog to be in high arousal constantly? (more on this later!)
- I need to use such a low rate of reinforcement or can the set-up be improved for more success?

If you make a frank appraisal of your training, adopting the "Do I need that?" attitude, you will be on your way to creating, developing and maintaining awesome behaviour without any negative consequences – and this applies equally to companion dogs and to performance dogs.

This attitude brings into question not only how we go about creating and developing behaviours for companionship and sport but also how to stop unwanted behaviours. Unwanted ("bad") is injurious to the relationship you share with your dog, as an unwanted behaviour in one area of life can affect and taint everything you do. From a sports perspective, a dog that is difficult to live with will mar the team effort. From a companionship point of view, unwanted behaviour can lead to a vicious cycle of an ever-diminishing relationship coupled with an ever-increasing level of inappropriate behaviour.

STOPPING UNWANTED BEHAVIOUR

With the learning tunnel framework in mind, we can consider two approaches to reducing the frequency of unwanted behaviour:

Option I

You could downgrade the tunnel of the behaviour you do not want until it is so dark, noisy, badly lit and uncomfortable that it doesn't get used. You may have to make it incredibly unaccommodating due to an element of habit being involved in the behaviour. In other words, the behaviour is not intrinsically rewarding and doesn't lead to reward, but your dog has always done it. In this situation, extremely aversive punishers may have to be used to change the dog's mindset.

Option II

Instead, you could focus on promoting and building a bypass straight past the tunnel in question, making it so comfortable, luxurious and easy-to-use that there is never any question over whether to use the inappropriate tunnel – life is just too great with the new tunnel.

This new tunnel represents an alternative behaviour. You can make the new tunnel one that is appropriate to the situation and incompatible with the old, inappropriate behaviour. For example, you would train a sit behaviour on greeting people rather than a jumping up behaviour; you would teach a stop contact behaviour rather than jumping over the contact behaviour, or you might train a down in the crate/on the mat behaviour rather than a zoomies around training class behaviour.

When training to reduce unwanted behaviour – a consequence of a choice we do not want our dogs to make – the "Do I need that" attitude forces us to question which option to use.

If you choose option 1, you will embark on a journey of using aversive tools and events on your dog, such as choke chains, intimidation, spray/shock collars. However, if you select option II, you can commence on a journey of enhancing, promoting and developing more appropriate tunnels. The secret is that there is always an alternative tunnel to enhance rather than attempting to destroy an unwanted tunnel.

This attitude is so powerful but sometimes it is difficult to decide on or even think of a 'good tunnel'. However, there is

TUNNEL OUTCOMES

Bad Tunnel (or choice)	Good Tunnel (or Choice)	Outcome
Pull on lead	Walk on lead offering regular eye contact!	Can't pull ahead as has value in eye contact, not possible if facing the other direction to pull
Countersurf	Lie on mat as soon as entering kitchen	Can't countersurf and lie on mat at the same time
Forging ahead or lagging behind in heelwork!	Target shoulder to my left leg	Can't forge or lag if targeting shoulder to left leg
Biting hands when playing with toy!	Bite specific bite area!	If biting specific target area, can't bite hands

Enhance the 'right' tunnel/choice, and your dog will be so delighted with the outcome that other tunnels/choices will disappear from view.

a trick to finding a good tunnel to build, which you can utilise by asking yourself the following questions:

What *do* I want?
Rather than what don't I want

What picture *do* I want to see?
Rather than what don't I want to see

Whenever you are presented with a behaviour you don't like, revisit these questions and you will immediately identify a tunnel to enhance and develop.

CHAPTER 4
TRAINING FOR FLEXIBILITY

Does your dog respond to the same situation in the same way every time? Or is he more flexible, adapting what he does and how he feels, depending on what is going on? A flexible response to a situation can be very useful, especially if you need to train multiple ways of interacting with the same object, or gaining a different response in a similar set-up. This could be:

- A running contact versus a stopped contact in agility.
- A recall to present versus a recall to finish in obedience.

For pet dogs, this might mean:

- Sometimes you go through a doorway first, sometimes you allow your dog to go first.
- Sometimes the tuggy lead is for tugging, sometimes it is for loose-lead walking.

There are also times when you want to change the way your dog has been behaving in relation to a specific environment or object. For example, if you want to put a stop to counter-surfing, in the kitchen, you first you need to build the skill of flexibility so that he is capable of responding differently to being near the kitchen counter.

There may also be situations when you want to change a response that is motivated by an emotion, which is often the case with reactive dogs. We cannot teach our dogs an alternative way to respond to a situation without first developing underlying flexibility as a concept. For example, we cannot train an 'orient to me calmly' response rather than a 'lunge and bark fearfully' response without first building flexibility. It's powerful.

This is why your dog needs to become a flexible learner – and flexibility, as a concept, is something I find increasingly important, the more I work with dogs.

The power of rehearsal in dog training means that with each rehearsal and with each repetition, the thought involved, and the choices available diminish, limiting the likelihood of a different response in the future. The choice the dog has made becomes more ingrained, and other available choices become less apparent. Counteracting this is the flexibility! In many of the cases I see and students I train, there is an underlying lack of flexibility that needs to be built and developed to overcome whatever struggle they may be facing.

GAMES TO PLAY

Object Tricks

This is a game that every dog should play, whatever his past and whatever his future career may be. It involves choosing an object, and then training a range of different behaviours with the object. Here are some examples:

Object: A stool/low platform

- One front or one back foot on.
- Both front or both back feet on.
- Front feet on and pivot to the left.
- Front feet on and pivot to the right.
- Back feet on and pivot to the left.
- Back feet on and pivot to the right.

- Rest chin.
- Front feet on and move to a sit.
- Front feet on and move to a bow.
- All four feet on.
- All four feet on and move back feet on to the floor.
- All four feet on and move front feet on to the floor.

And so on...there is no end to the variations you can introduce.

Object: A spoon (or a hand!)

- Target nose to spoon.
- Target left front paw, right front paw, left hind paw or right hind paw to spoon.
- Target chin, shoulder or hip to spoon.
- Hold spoon.
- Hold spoon and do behaviours.
- Pick up spoon.
- Stand on spoon.
- Retrieve spoon.

And so on...

Reward Anything

This is one of my favourite games! It builds flexibility, creativity, motivation, the ability to think through arousal and frustration productively, and provides fun in your training sessions. You can use it as a warm-up before a session, or simply play it as a game in its own right. Here's how it works:

- Reward your dog for offering any behaviour or movement. Aim for these movements to be as tiny as possible, as well as offering of tricks that you have trained specifically.

- You are not allowed to reward the same behaviour more than once.
- Be careful not to reward behaviour chains, i.e. series of the same behaviours over and over again in a pattern.

The game is for the dog to offer varied behaviours, but he needs to be sufficiently thoughtful so as not offer the same behaviours twice in a row, and to offer different responses to the same situation – flexibility!

If your dog is struggling with this game, it may be that you are looking for too much and failing to reward tiny behaviours (think slight movement of right paw, and then next time, slight movement of left paw, for example). Or you may need to play the game using objects first (see below).

Reward Anything With Objects

This is exactly the same game as the reward anything game, but with an object involved. This game is great for beginners as an object prompts offering of behaviour. The object can be anything from a book to a pole or a food bowl.

Me Tricks

This game follows the same principle as object tricks, except the object is you! Training your dog to interact with you, in as many different ways as possible, is a great way of developing focus, enhancing your relationship and, at the same time, building flexibility.

Here are some of the behaviours you can train:

- Leg weaves (both directions) – your dog does a figure of eight around your legs.
- Circle – your dog circles your entire body.
- Middle – your dog sits, stands or lies down between your legs (you can do this with your dog going backwards, too).

- Heel on left and right – your dog targets his shoulder to your left or right leg.

And these are just to get started with...

PRACTICE!

This is probably the most important aspect of flexibility training. The more you change the way your dog usually interacts with objects, the easier it will become in the future. Changing the way he behaves in certain situations, or in response to certain things, enhances his learning so that he becomes an adaptable and flexible individual.

THE VALUE OF REWARD SWITCHING

Variety in the way you reward your dog is incredibly enriching to both dog and trainer. Dogs find variety more reinforcing than the same old reward, and variety in your training means you can more effectively choose a reward to suit the situation. For example, it may not be appropriate to reward your dog with a tennis ball in a café or to use a squeaky toy in a training class.

The key to success with reinforcer variety is to avoid what I term 'reinforcer disappointment'. Reward switching is, in itself, a type of flexibility we want to develop with dogs – same situation but the reward is different – and it's still rewarding and exciting.

Reinforcer Disappointment

If your dog doesn't get what he is expecting in your reinforcement strategy, he can actually find it punishing – the opposite to what you intend.

In 2013, I did a study to discover whether dogs that were scared of loud noises had a more pessimistic or a more optimistic outlook. It was based on a simple game where the dog would approach a bowl that was placed in different locations. When the bowl was in a specific location it would contain food; when placed in other locations, it would be empty.

Alongside the main findings, the game revealed an unexpected outcome. It showed that dogs were more punished when they expected a reward (i.e. when the bowl was closest to the location where they had previously found food) and failed to get it, compared with anticipating no reward and being correct that there was, indeed, no reward.

This is something that has become increasingly apparent in my clinical experience when working with dogs' emotions and behavioural problems. Unexpected outcomes are incredibly punishing to dogs – far greater than the punishing effect of the outcome itself when it is expected. This is something I call 'the disappointment effect'. It highlights why it is so important to build value in many reinforcers so that you have the choice of what best fits the situation. But, just as importantly, you need to further build value in switching between them so that your dog is not being punished by your choice of reinforcer.

GAMES TO PLAY

There are a number of games you can play with your dog that are key to developing his ability to switch between reinforcers:

Toy Switching

- Switch between toys by animating the one your dog is not currently playing with. Keep practising until he will happily switch between any toy. You can play this game with a variety of different toys from your dog's favourite to his least favourite.
- The key to the game is to start by switching upwards in value (less liked toy to more liked toy). Then as learning develops, make it more difficult and ask your dog to switch from a higher value toy to a lower value toy. When you are switching from higher to lower value toys, make sure to reinforce this 'good choice' by immediately switching back to the toy that has higher value.

Reward Switching

- Switch between toy and food, and back to toy, by animating the one your dog is not currently interacting with.
- Work on switching between toy and food outside of training sessions and then practise in your training sessions. This takes the same form as the toy switching game, but incorporates toys and food.
- You can spice it up by adding variety to the food and toys you are using.

Race to the Bowl

- This game involves setting up a bowl ahead of your dog, placing a reward inside the bowl and then racing your dog to the bowl. Each time you do it, change the reinforcer.
- The race to the bowl builds anticipation and generally makes the dog keen to switch between different types of rewards.

RACE TO THE BOWL

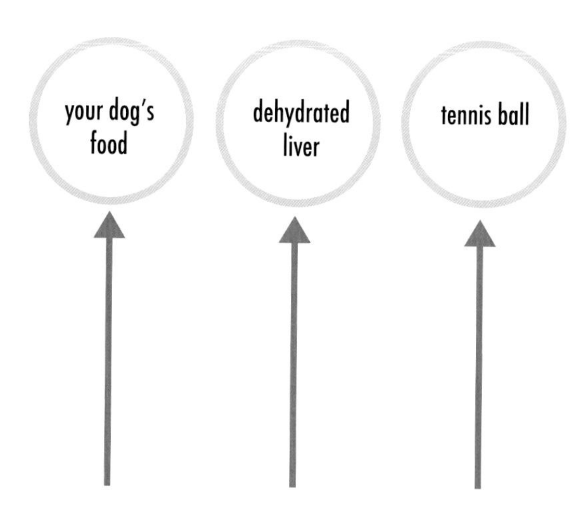

A game that builds anticipation as the dog switches between different rewards.

CHAPTER 5
THINKERS AND DOERS

We work with a wide variety of dogs, differing in breed, type and training history. But we have discovered a more subtle difference – and this is in the way dogs make choices. Some dogs are more likely to opt for stillness/duration while others will opt for movement. Some stand back and are more cautious in their decision-making; others will be impulsive and jump into situations all guns blazing.

Looking at a range of scenarios, I would divide dogs into thinkers and doers. Each dog lies on a spectrum from extreme thinker to extreme doer; where he lies on the spectrum influences the choices he makes and the way in which he makes those choices. The outcome for each of these types may be identical, but the way in which a dog prioritises understanding, speed and intensity in his learning and choices will vary considerably.

Thinkers prioritise full understanding of the 'rules' – the criteria of the training/situation – and then add in speed and intensity once they have everything sussed. Doers typically add in speed and intensity right from the word go and are typically high arousal learners. If you have an extreme thinker or, at the other end of the spectrum, an extreme doer, training can be challenging, regardless of whether you are working for companionship or performance. Thinkers may be described as hesitant while doers may be described as hasty. The real struggles with thinkers versus doers typically presents when

THINKERS AND DOERS

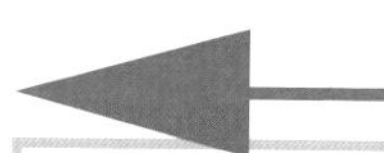

Whether your dog is predominantly a thinker or a doer will influence the ways he behaves.

a trainer is unaware of the dog's learning style, or the dog's learning style is incompatible with the training style of the trainer. This becomes a case of fitting a square peg into a round hole which, inevitably, leads to frustration.

Crucial to success in working with this concept is having an honest understanding of what best suits your personality, and your natural training style. For example, does hesitation frustrate you more than hastiness? Once you have taken this on board, the next step is to consider where your dog sits on the spectrum from extreme thinker to extreme doer. Finally, you need to work out how to adapt your training and expectations to suit your dog, while you are developing the personality traits that best suits his situation.

FINDING THE BALANCE

There is a piece of advice I frequently use in training seminars, which states:

> *"It is the teacher's function to contrive conditions under which students learn. Their relevance to a future usefulness need not be obvious."*
>
> **B.F. Skinner, *The Free & Happy Student*, 1973**

In this context, it implies that the trainer needs to change what he is doing. I acknowledge this, but I think we can take it one step further. We also need to develop the dog's skills so he can best tackle a situation, in this case, balancing him as a thinker/doer. It should be our aim to enhance a dog's personality to fit him for his intended role.

Identify what you have in front of you: a thinker or a doer. Once you have done that, you can then work to promote attributes of thinking and doing to match what you want, and the job that is ahead. All sports require a balance to some degree and companionship certainly does. You are now in a position to prioritise your training to accommodate your goals. You still train everything to a thinker and a doer, but the order in which you do it is key!

For example, if you want to make your dog more thoughtful, you would prioritise adding duration to his basic positions (sit, down, stand), rather than focusing on fast-paced transitions between them. Equally you may prioritise the performance of precise and accurate tricks, such as nose targets and paw targets or placing four feet in a small box, rather than concentrating on fast-paced, movement-oriented tricks, such as leg weaves and spins.

Your reinforcement strategy can also influence the direction in which you push your dog down the spectrum. For example, marking and rewarding the movement into a position, rather than marking and rewarding once the position has been adopted, can have a huge impact on the skills you are developing in your dog.

CHANGE IT

THINKERS

DOERS

push towards thinker:
adding position duration
movement-orientated tricks
mark and reward end position

push towards doer:
prioritise position changes
movement-orientated tricks
reward anything
mark and reward the movement to position

There are simple ways to change your dog's natural way of thinking.

Personally, I prefer working with dogs that are more doers than thinkers; this suits their role as demonstration dogs when I am teaching. Now that I have a good understanding of this concept, I actively build my dogs into being doers very early on in their training, building this trait which may, or may not, have been evident when selecting them as puppies.

For example, I identified Lava, my young Standard Poodle puppy, as more of a thinker very early on, as was her mother. I chose her from the litter for other characteristics that suited my multi-dog household dynamic at that time, such as her flexibility and tolerance of frustration. But I knew that developing her as a doer would be a priority in her early training.

Practically, this meant ditching her typical default behaviours, such as sits, downs and stays, and instead, taking a 'doer' approach, focusing on movement and transitions. This is the order in which I prioritised training of behaviours in the first couple of months:

- Left spin.
- Middle position with immediate release (moving around my body to stood position in between my legs).
- Run to a target and place a foot on it.
- Right spin.
- Run around a pole.
- Reverse on to a target.

Notice that I concentrated on teaching a limited number of behaviours – fewer than some trainers might work on in the first two months of owning a dog. Why was that? It was because the use of behaviours was not the focus; it was rather developing in Lava the concept of becoming a doer. I needed to focus on quality over quantity, and work on creating a learner that would suit her job in such a way that future training would be a cinch.

Work out whether you are pushing your dog to be more of a thinker or a doer by calculating the percentage of their time that is occupied by each type of work. You would become more of a thinker if you filled your time with crosswords and Sudoku, but probably you would become more of a doer if you filled your time with formula one racing and mountain biking, where hesitation isn't an option.

Remember, being a doer is not necessarily the most desirable for all dogs. A dog's individual personality needs to suit his job, and more thought is required in a lot of jobs.

Regardless of whether your dog is a thinker or a doer, you should be aware that this concept is powerful. It allows you to have an even more dynamic relationship with your dog because it is completely fluid, allowing you to adapt to each other and to the job at hand.

CHAPTER 6
TRAINING THROUGH INSPIRATION NOT DEPRIVATION

In simple terms, this entails creating dogs that are highly susceptible to reinforcement from their owners/trainers through inspiration rather than deprivation. Dogs that highly susceptible to reinforcement from their *owners/trainers* are described as "driven", "keen", or "motivated". In contrast, dogs that are highly susceptible to reinforcement from the *environment* are typically termed "stubborn", "difficult", "disinterested".

In his book, *The Evolution of Behaviour* (1984), Burrhus Frederic Skinner frequently acknowledged that an animal's trainability (in his work, mostly relating to the way animals adapt to their environment) comes down to the individual's susceptibility to reinforcement, i.e. how easily he/she can be rewarded. Skinner proposes that it is susceptibility to reinforcement, for example, the tendency to be rewarded by food, that is inherited and gives certain individuals an advantage over others, rather than inheriting the learning itself. This gives certain individuals a selective advantage over others in changing environments where learning of one generation may not be useful in the next, for example in the search for food.

I like this explanation in dog training for two reasons:

Firstly, it acknowledges that some animals are more

trainable than others – and this relates to their readiness to respond to rewards. Susceptibility to reward is a concept – just like focus, flexibility and decision-making, which we have already discussed – and the great thing about concepts is that they can be enhanced. This is exciting! It means we can make our dogs ever more trainable...

Secondly, it highlights the fact that the dogs that may be deemed the most "untrainable" – dogs who sniff every scent, meet and greet every dog in the park, steal from the kitchen counter or take any agility obstacle on a whim – are, by definition, the most trainable. This type of dog is very, very susceptible to reinforcement; it is simply that he is not using the rewards we have in mind and is, instead, taking environmental rewards very readily, and without involvement from us.

Taking on board these two points, we can:

- Make every dog a reward junkie.
- Make those that are already reward junkies, the most trainable dogs possible and, even more importantly, we can make their rewards entirely appropriate. The distractions that were seen as negatives can be harnessed and enhanced so that they become rewards.

Reward-based training relies on the use of rewards and while many of us embark on the journey of training our dogs using rewards and the practice of positive reinforcement, we often lack an understanding of:

- How to create a dog that is susceptible to this process.
- How to create a dog that finds an infinite number of things rewarding.
- How to harness the power of life events and move from competing against distractions to working in unison with them.
- How to embrace reward-based dog training rather than tinkering with it and making do with poor results.

REINFORCING AND REWARDING

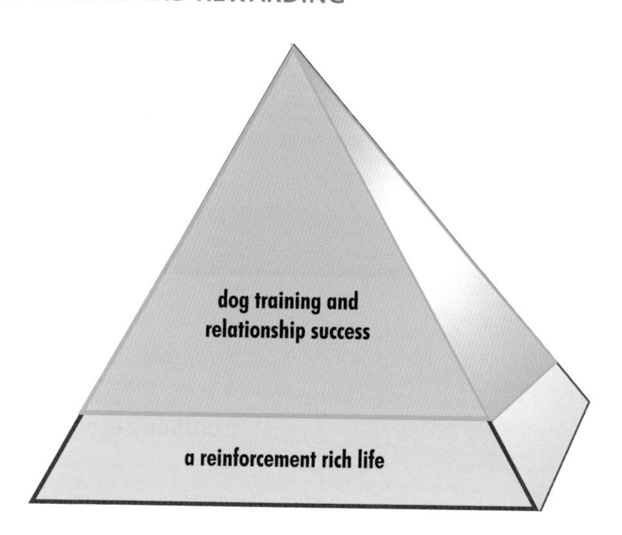

A dog's susceptibility to rewards affects his whole outlook on life.

At the basis of each of the above is the reinforcement-rich life framework.

As previously discussed, a dog will progress through each day making choices based on whether those choices have been rewarded in the past. You may have been instrumental in rewarding these choices, for example, rewarding a sit on cue in a training session. Or the reward may have come from an unscheduled event or opportunity, such as surfing the kitchen counter and finding a sandwich.

In many instances, the reward may seem innocuous – your dog ignores a recall for a couple of seconds because he has just spotted a friend across the park. However, his 'ignore the recall' choice has been rewarded, making that brain tunnel more likely to be selected in the future. The key message is that our dogs will go through life being reinforced for choices whether we take control of choices/reinforcement or not.

However, if you see these events as opportunities that you can harness and reward, behaviours such as jumping on the sofa, pulling on the lead, running around the field like a mad thing, or access to any desirable event for that matter, becomes an event you can use to promote other tunnels. It puts you back in the driving seat, giving you the means to achieve training success on your terms, rather than allowing your dog to self-train – and self-reward.

This is not to say that we advocate limiting and restricting access to things your dog finds enjoyable. In a safe environment, such as in the house, my dogs have the freedom to make any and every choice they wish. Dogs go through life loving things and accessing the things they love, so it makes perfect sense for us to get involved with the preferences they show, and use them as rewards when the opportunities present themselves.

This has big consequences with regard to the relationship you share with your dog. Imagine your relationship as a bank account. To invest and pay into this relationship bank account, you need a positive interaction with your dog, i.e. you need to do something fun that he clearly likes. The more he values (or likes) the event, the more he buys into the bank account, and the investment placed in the relationship grows accordingly. By taking control of – and making use of – every fun and pleasant event in your dog's life, you are feeding his entire world into your relationship bank account. What does this mean? Super relationship!

For dog trainers, this is incredibly exciting as it means you can go from being a bystander in your dog's life, attempting to compete with distractions, to feeding these distracting events/objects/things into your relationship bank account. In addition, you are working on all your training aims – whether that's a recall, a difficult weave entry or fun fitness exercises and tricks. It makes every single dog immensely trainable!

WHAT DETERMINES THE VALUE OF A REWARD?

If your dog perceives little or no value in a variety of different rewards, getting the most in learning and performance from him will be next to impossible. When you are creating any behaviour (positions, mat/crate games, retrieves, recall, contacts, etc.), in terms of reinforcement you will get out as much as you put in. So how do you determine the value of a reward?

A dog uses a number of factors to work out what he considers most valuable/desirable. These include:

- His inherent like or desire for the event/item/resource – e.g. 'foodie dogs'.
- Abundance of opportunity for that event/item/resource – e.g. dogs that have bowls of food down at all times often don't value food at all.
- Amount of work required to achieve it – e.g. animals often seem to experience more enjoyment from items they have worked hard to get due to the anticipatory effect. They prefer food gained with effort, which is termed 'contra-freeloading'.
- Previous learning, in other words, whether there have been any previous enhancements to the associated tunnel with that rewarding behaviour – e.g. grabbing the toy leads to tugging with the toy.

These determining factors are intrinsic to learning in all animal species. They are based on a principle known as 'resource-holding potential', and can be used in your dog training for better results. As already stated, a reinforcement-rich life does not need to involve deprivation, i.e. restricting your dog's access to resources such as food, off lead exercise, or freedom from his crate.

Realistically, these events are going to happen regardless – you will always feed your dog, let him have free time, allow him to go exploring and greet people and other dogs – so you may as well use these highly rewarding events in your training. In fact, based on the principle of contra-freeloading, your dog will enjoy them more, giving you a win, win situation!

INSPIRATION NOT DEPRIVATION

By working with everyday events in your dog's life, you can enhance his desires – and make it work for you:

Attaching the lead prior to a walk	➡	Ask for a chain of sits, downs and stands first
Releasing for zoomies around the field	➡	Ask for a 'middle' position (see page 152)
Letting your dog off-lead	➡	Wait for eye contact, before letting him off
Greeting a visitor at home	➡	Ask for a two-on, two-off position on the bottom of the stairs
Jumping up on the sofa	➡	Wait for eye contact, then cue to sofa
Release to free running	➡	Play tug with his toy, then send
Release to go swimming	➡	Do some leg weaves and then send
Eating dinner	➡	Ask for behaviour chains, pole wrapping, shaping games, you name it
Playing with toys	➡	Ask for a nose target and then send to toy

Playing with other dogs	Recall your dog and then send him to play Ask him to leg weave and then send him Ask for "middle" and then send him
Greeting other dogs	Ask for eye contact and then allow him to greet
Greeting people	Ask for a nose target and allow him to greet Ask to come to heel and then greet
Release to the garden	Ask for control position at the door to then release to garden

Utilise what is rewarding for your dog and pay it into the relationship bank account

TURNING DISTRACTION INTO SUCCESS

Now as we discovered, our dogs are continually telling us what they find reinforcing because they are doing it! Every time your dog...

- Takes a jump in favour of the weaves.
- Leaves you in training class to greet another dog.
- Runs off in the park in pursuit of a scent.
- Chooses a game of chase with another dog rather than coming back to you.

...he is giving you a message, loud and clear! Your job is to watch and learn – and then do something with the information. These are highly reinforcing behaviours to your dog, but if you can make use of them in your training, there will be no stopping you. The question is how? This is where the "ok go" cue comes in.

IT'S OK TO GO!

The "ok go" cue does just that! It signals to your dog that the choice he just made was brilliant; you are now cueing him to go and perform a high value behaviour in the environment as his reward! That high value behaviour may be racing to a food bowl or a toy that you placed, or it may be chasing the rabbit that is running across the field, or going to say hello to the dog in the park.

You are using the "ok go" cue to send him to something he really wants as a reward. As a consequence, the value transfers from that exciting event to the behaviour and choice you want to build and reinforce. Over time, the behaviour you want to promote becomes more likely to happen, and the behaviour that used to be a distraction (the rabbit, the dog, the scents, etc.) become less likely – the value transfers! The proof is when your dog ups his game in the midst of distractions, or comes sprinting back to you in favour of chasing a rabbit!

The key is training the "ok go" cue – and you can start working on this at home:

Stage 1

- Find a high value reward, such as tasty food or an exciting toy, and place it on the ground.
- Restrain your dog and when you give the verbal cue: "ok go", release him to his reward.
- Repeat this until your dog pulls towards the reward after hearing the verbal cue, in anticipation of being sent.
- At this point, I would introduce a variety of rewards, and start training out and about on walks.

Stage 2

- This time, place the reward close by so you can reach for it. Restrain your dog briefly, let go – then give your verbal cue, "ok go".
- If your dog moves before you give the cue, simply cover the food or toy with your hand. Wait for him to adopt a control position (stillness in a sit, down or stand) and then give the "ok go" cue.
- Build up duration before giving the verbal cue. You can help your dog to stay calm and focus by stroking him down the side a couple of times and then giving the cue.

Stage 3

- Finally, ask for cued behaviours, for example, sit, down or spin, and then reward with "ok go!"
- When you are teaching your dog "ok, go", use a reliable cued behaviour that your dog values – but not your dog's favourite behaviour. This keeps him on-task rather than anticipating and performing off-cue in the presence of the distraction (the food bowl, for example). Do this everywhere and with everything!
- When you start asking for cued behaviours before releasing to the distraction, make sure to regularly revisit stages one and two to stop the game becoming high pressure or boring for your dog. You can never go wrong topping up the value of the "ok go" cue and, should the framework ever fall apart, it is typically because stages one and two need a top-up.
- Use the "ok go" as a confidence-building, distraction-busting warm-up in new environment. For example, play it during the course of a walk on a random basis, or at the start of a training class.

Now that you have truly unlocked and determined what your dog finds reinforcing, you can use these behaviours and activities for the behaviours you want to reinforce and work on, building new and different reinforcers that are suitable for different situations.

BUILDING REINFORCERS

You have reached a point when you can transfer the value between behaviours by following the lower value behaviour with the higher value behaviour as already discussed. This could be a down followed by a tug game, or a retrieve followed by chase the ball or a recall followed by an "ok go" to race another dog.

You can also build reinforcers, too. Over time, you can build an arsenal of reinforcers – each one suitable for a specific situation – which will become crucial to your success as a trainer. They will also provide variety, excitement and surprise when you are interacting with your dog.

PROTOCOL FOR REINFORCER DEVELOPMENT *Here is a protocol for developing reinforcers:*
1. Create and promote the behaviour that you want to enhance, and therefore use as a reinforcer, in preference to your dog's 'go to' choice. For example, engage your dog with a toy, and build chase into the game, or roll food on the floor to create added interest.
2. This is work in progress, so first get your dog to interact with his reward – a touch of the toy or nibble of the food is fine at this stage. You may need to animate the reward to make it more exciting, or you can incorporate arousal cues, e.g. "Reaaady", to build anticipation.
3. As soon as you see any sort of interaction, surprise your dog with the opportunity to perform a behaviour he prefers, such as running with you, eating, chasing a ball, or tugging with a toy.

Then remove the item/suspend the interaction. Surprise is powerful and is crucial to success both at this stage and in achieving overall success with this protocol. If you are failing to make progress, you can guarantee that it's because you are not harnessing the surprise element!

4. *It may be that you will not be able to get a repeat of the lower value behaviour (e.g. grabbing the toy or nibbling the food) so end the session and be ready to surprise him in your next training session.*

5. *Continue working on pairing the lower value behaviour with the higher value, and, over time, the value will transfer to the behaviour that was previously deemed to be low value. Work on this a couple of times a day in short, sharp bursts.*

TOP TIP!

For super success, make the contingency between the behaviours. What do I mean by this?

As long as it is safe, fair and feasible, you need to make sure that the only time your dog gets to do the higher value behaviour is after he has performed the lower value behaviour.

For example, let's say you are building value for tugging by transferring value from chasing a tennis ball, which is your dog's preferred behaviour. In this scenario, the only time the tennis ball is produced is after your dog has played tug, i.e. after he has performed the lower value behaviour.

CREATIVE REINFORCER DEVELOPMENT

Now that you have this protocol, you can take anything and build it as a reinforcer – and this gives the opportunity to be really smart with what you build. You can move away from a world where you are limited to using food and toys in training and embrace a new world where there are infinite reinforcer opportunities. This will not only benefit your training, it will enhance your relationship with your dog.

Regardless of whether you are training pet obedience, or a competitive sport, the biggest concern, voiced by dog owners, is what can you do when you are in a situation where you do not have access to the reinforcer you generally use? What do you do when you can't take food/toy into the competition ring, or you have forgotten to take your treats to the park?

Do not despair! Finding a solution starts at the level of reinforcer development. You need to develop reinforcers beyond eating and playing with a toy, and expand your repertoire of reinforcers so you always have one to hand.

Additional reinforcers could be:

- Clapping your hands.
- Getting your dog to chase you.
- Giving your dog physical contact.
- Catching grass you throw into the air.
- Engaging in push play – pushing your dog away from you and encouraging him to bounce back in.

You can be as creative as you like – it's all about using your body and things readily available, and not needing to rely on very specific props. You have transferred the value to something that is always around, so a clap of your hands can reward a super recall in the park, or a push on the chest will reward your dog for a job well done in the competition ring. The beauty of this is you are never left without a reinforcer because you are standing there with limbs intact – and no judge can fault you for that!

CHAPTER 7
TRAINING FOR GENERALISATION

The skill of generalisation is crucial to developing a successful team. It affects how quickly and how readily learning of a behaviour can be applied to a new situation, i.e. a situation or an environment that differs from the one in which the behaviour was first learnt. This concept may govern either a behavioural or an emotional response. For example, it might be getting that perfect recall in the park that you always have at home, or getting that calm and positive emotional response that you have developed when your dog sees black Labradors transferred to all black dogs or, even, all dogs. The ability to generalise, therefore, has important consequences for our dogs.

A dog's aptitude in terms of generalising can be a determining factor in both positive and negative experiences. For example,

GENERALISATION

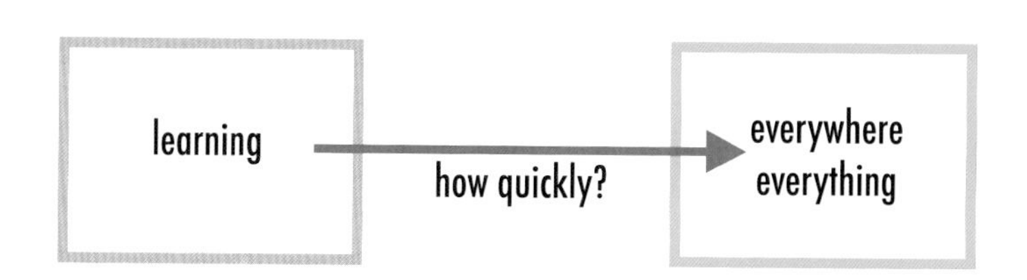

The ability to take learning to different places can be nurtured.

your dog may readily learn that everything is good from a positive experience, such as being given food when he sees a car for the first time generalising to all vehicles including trains and lorries meaning food! Equally, he may be quick to learn from a bad experience and generalise it, resulting in a negative association.

This stark difference in ability to generalise is very apparent in dogs that have been attacked by a Border Collie, for example. Some will develop a negative association specific to Border Collies, some to black and white dogs, some to large dogs in general and some to all dogs – this is the full spectrum of generalisation ability. It also impacts on how well your dog is able to take cued behaviours, whether it be a recall or a stopped contact, to new places. Finally, generalisation plays a role in how the value that you have built into food, a toy or other reinforcer translates into everyday life and different environments.

GENERALISTION IN ACTION

The pros and cons of good generalisers

good	bad
trained behaviours everywhere quickly value everywhere quickly positive associations everywhere quickly	unwanted behaviours everywhere quickly negative associations everywhere quickly

There can be drawbacks when a dog is a good generaliser – but these are outweighed by the advantages.

There are pros and cons to being a good generaliser but, on the whole, developing your dog to be a keen generaliser is beneficial in getting consistent behaviour in both companion and sports dogs, and is also helpful in overcoming behavioural problems.

You may be familiar with generalising a behaviour, which entails making a behaviour consistent in different environments, and certainly you can do this for each and every behaviour. However, generalisation is a skill in itself and the more you develop it, the less you need to work on generalising individual behaviours, associations and values as your dog is able to do it automatically.

GAMES TO PLAY

There are a number of games which will help your dog to become a skillful generaliser:

The Generalisation Game

The generalisation game is so much fun for you and your dog! In this game, you train your dog to interact with an object in a specific way, for example rewarding him for putting his front feet on a stool. You then throw a piece of food away from him and, before he returns, you switch the object to something similar but different. For example, you might switch the stool for a wobble cushion, an upturned food bowl, or a book.

You can adapt this game to nose targeting (start with a spoon, and progress to spatulas, books, sticks, bottles, etc.), and to retrieve (getting your dog to retrieve a series of articles which could include a dumbbell, a toy, a spoon, or even an egg!).

Portable Tricks

Portable tricks are a gift! These are tricks that involve a strong visual cue, for example, an object such as a paw pod, that you can take to new environments and communicate to your dog that the learning at home is the same as the learning everywhere else. When training my young dog, Betcha, one of the first exercises I taught her was to place her front feet on a paw pod. Wherever we went, the paw pod came as well – and when I placed it on the ground, she hopped on. I then did the same with her pole wrapping behaviour, first teaching her to wrap a pole and then taking it different places. I then asked her to wrap 'natural poles', such as trees, lamp posts, traffic cones, etc.

This is a really powerful message to train a dog – you simply can't do enough of it! It not only teaches your dog that the learning goes everywhere and is applied to everything, it also shows him that new and strange environments are safe and can be manipulated and interacted with, just as at home – and this equals confidence!

Pole Wrapping

Pole wrapping is such a valuable behaviour to train, I use it in my training – and throughout this book – as a vital communicator of many concepts. Pole wrapping involves your dog running around a pole or barrel single or multiple times on cue. Dogs generally love this behaviour!

This is how I teach it:

- Start by building confidence with being close to the chosen object. You can do this by getting your dog to chase a toy or food around a barrel.
- Begin shaping the wrap. To do this, mark and reward any step towards or around the object. Build this up slowly, over many sessions, until your dog is comfortable offering wrapping the barrel in either direction.
- Once this is reliable, and your dog has a lot of value in both directions, reward a single direction only

a few times. When you are confident that your dog is going to offer wrapping the barrel in that direction, give your verbal cue and then release him from a restrain. Repeat this until the cue is learnt.

- Now add a cue to the other direction.
- Remember to incorporate this behaviour into the generalisation game (see page 93).

In addition to front feet on and pole wrapping, the portable tricks I use include:

- Platform work, in which your dog places four feet on a platform. You can choose to cue behaviour chains of sit, down, stand, etc., while on the platform, too.
- Boundary games, in which your dog calmly settles on a boundary (crate, raised bed, box) until released
- Retrieve of favourite retrieve article, typically a dumbbell for my dogs.

Reshape

This is a game I employ when I need to:

- Build the skill of generalisation, whether that is a companion dog that needs consistency between environments or a sports dog that struggles to transfer learning to the competition ring.
- Build thought and learning ability in an exciting/arousing environment.
- Build optimism, especially in naughty but nice dogs or dogs whose speed/intensity is environmentally sensitive.

Reshaping is a term I made up; it simply means starting from scratch, shaping something that your dog already knows. For example, you may have trained your dog to place four feet in a box at home, so you go to a new environment and start from scratch and shape the behaviour all over again. The choices (tunnels) have already been primed and enhanced to make his choice easier and more instant. In turn, you will be ready to reward his choice – maybe starting with just one foot on the box – to increase his confidence and further develop the value in that choice tunnel.

I cannot recommend this process enough – it is truly powerful! Do this with your recalls, your boundary games (where your dog has to stay in a designated area until released), your agility contact training, your obedience positions – do it with everything!

PRACTICE MAKES PERFECT!

As with most aspects of training, the more you generalise behaviours, associations and values, the easier it will be for your dog to do it in the future. Practise, practise, practise!

CHAPTER 8
TRUE GRIT!

This may be the first time you have heard of 'grit' as a training concept. It is a recent addition to my training repertoire – but through training my dogs and my students' dogs, I have discovered that it makes all the difference! Investigating this concept in human psychology has become widespread and I anticipate that canine research will soon follow suit.

Let's start by looking at the definition of grit given by Angela Duckworth and her research team:

> *"Grit is the tendency to sustain interest in and effort toward very long-term goals."*
>
> **Duckworth et al., 2007**

In dog training terms, I translate this as being the ability of some individuals to work for less frequent or longer-term rewards. Of course this is, in part, influenced by other traits such as self-control, tolerance of frustration and being able to learn and perform when aroused. However, as reflected in human research, the links between these traits are not consistent, with some humans being extremely gritty but lacking self-control, and vice versa *(Duckworth & Gross, 2014)*. I am sure you can appreciate that this occurs in dogs, too.

An extreme example is the dog who will work and work and work without reward, in anticipation of the food in front of him. But, given half the chance, he will forget the work and snatch the food off cue! In humans, there is evidence to show that, in the long-term, grit is much more crucial to success and performance than intelligence (*Duckworth, A. L. & Seligman, M. E. P., 2005*). With regard to sports dogs, 'gritty' dogs are generally more successful, and the same is true of companion, therapy and service dogs who seem better able to fulfill the job at hand.

At the present time, it is difficult to know for certain whether this concept works the same way in dogs as it does in humans. However, training our dogs the concept of working for longer term goals (or rewards) is incredibly useful. It automatically boosts skills such as:

- Duration.
- Working without reward.
- Reliability of behaviours in everyday life.
- Calmness, patience, and household manners.

GAMES TO PLAY

I have devised a number of games which will help you to build and develop grit:

Short-Term GOOD, Long-Term BETTER

This game teaches your dog that low value rewards come quickly, but the best ones come when working for longer. It teaches him that working for longer, whether that is duration of behaviours, duration of a run, or being calm and polite in the house, leads to better rewards!

To play this, you need a very high value reward – think of the best toy or the tastiest treat – and a low value reward, such as bland kibble.

- Ask for a chain of behaviours, rewarding regularly with the kibble.
- Now ask for a series of behaviours (sit, down, stand, spin left), depending on your dog's repertoire, and reward this

longer chain with the super high value reward.

- Play the same game with duration. Ask for a duration behaviour, for example a sit or down, and reward frequently with the low value treat.
- Increase duration and then surprise him with the high value reward.

Race to Food/Toy: "Show Me You Want It"

This is a game I start to play with puppies quite early on, especially when I identify that they lack grit. This involves throwing a toy or piece of food ahead of the pup while he is restrained. He is only released to the toy/food for doing something – this might be a stare at the food/toy, a push against your hand or a wiggle.

After playing this a few times, begin to want for more and more from the pup so he is "working" harder before being released. Wait until he is really pushing against the restraint, and even barking at the food/toy saying: "I want it!"

This is a great grit game – just be careful not to overdo it.

Race to Food/Toy: Assault Courses

This is a great grit builder. It involves restraining your dog and throwing a piece of food or toy out as before. But this time, you are going to release him right away and then race him to the food/toy.

From here, you can build up the degree of difficulty, which involves increasing the effort/grit the dog has to put in to reach their goal. You can do this in the following ways:

- Increasing the distance the food/toy is thrown.
- Beating him to the food/toy to add in competition (if you can!).
- Setting up barriers between your dog and the food/toy, for example, jump poles, corners, etc.

- Throwing the food/toy into a container – an upturned barrel, for example.
- Throwing the food/toy into water.

...the variations are endless.

> ***TOP TIP!***
>
> *Grit is like a muscle – the more your dog uses it, the bigger and stronger it will become! This means you need to make sure you set your dog up for success and ensure he never practises giving up, tiring or refusing. He should always be powering ahead, pushing harder to reach his goal.*

Boundary Games

These are games where your dog has to stay in a designated area until he is released – this may be a mat, a crate, a tent, a platform – you name it! They are great for building grit because the dog learns:

- To work consistently in order to achieve long-term goals – this could be getting a piece of kibble on the boundary, or being released to play agility.
- To work more for less reward in lower arousal, which will transfer to higher arousal contexts where grit can be especially crucial, for example in the dog park, in training, or in competition.

So what do boundary games look like and what criteria do they involve? To your dog they mean:

- Go to this area (whether it is a mat, a crate, a raised table, a chair, etc.) on cue.
- Stay in this area and remain calm.
- Do not move from the area until you hear the release cue.

- The release cue means leave the area and interact with your owner/trainer.

This seems pretty straightforward – but boundary games communicate and train lots of concepts and skills, which include:

- Promoting and developing impulse control.
- Increasing motivation in your training sessions.
- Decreasing arousal by building calmness into the behaviour – boundaries become portable calmness switches when needed!
- Cleaning up your training sessions.

The rules of the game also communicate specific concepts to your dog, which include:

- When he leaves an area, he orients to, and works with, you.
- He can switch off (lower arousal) and then switch back on (high-arousal) when you signal.
- Some areas and distractions may be out of bounds – and that's a good thing.
- His release cue means go interact with something fun (and that fun thing is you most of the time) unless you signal otherwise.

It is easy to see that in training the simple rules of the game, you are able to convey so many other messages to your dog. And, with a little help, they can be generalised to a variety of situations. That's pretty special!

This game is magical when it comes to arousal. In my experience, it pitches nearly every dog's arousal levels at their optimum point – that sweet spot of peak learning and performance. It applies to all the skills you want to train but, in my opinion, its effects on grit are huge – both from the perspective of training and living in harmony with your dog.

The game says: *good things are coming – they might be a while away – but it's so worth working for them*. This applies equally to a game of tug at the end of a super speedy agility run, or a walk at the end of the day after being well behaved and calm in the house.

Training boundary games is loads of fun; I start training by using a mat and the process of shaping. However, some trainers prefer to use a crate, especially where dogs are quite frantic shapers (or "doers") and approach learning new skills with very high arousal. We need to avoid this becoming a high arousal behaviour; there needs to be an intrinsic calmness associated with it.

Here's a sample shaping plan for starting mat games:

- Reward looking at the mat.
- Reward stepping towards the mat.
- Reward stepping on to the mat.
- Reward two feet on the mat.
- Reward three/four feet on the mat and place reward low to the ground to aid your dog in offering the next stage, which is a down.
- Reward a weight shift back while on the mat and place reward low again.
- Reward a weight shift back that leads to rear hitting ground while on the mat and place reward low.
- Reward duration.
- Reward duration, say release cue (e.g. "free"/"release"/ "break") and throw the reward away from the mat to promote moving off.

Turn-Taking

If you live in a multi-dog household, how do you interact, train, run, work with one of your dogs while the others settle/control themselves waiting for their turn? The game of turn-taking has many useful applications – and it certainly increases a dog's grit/desire to work.

Take a look at the true grit recipe, I have devised to see how it works.

TRUE GRIT RECIPE

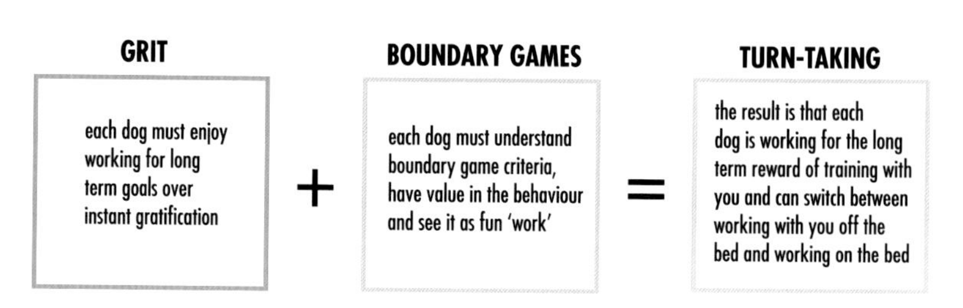

GRIT
each dog must enjoy working for long term goals over instant gratification
+
BOUNDARY GAMES
each dog must understand boundary game criteria, have value in the behaviour and see it as fun 'work'
=
TURN-TAKING
the result is that each dog is working for the long term reward of training with you and can switch between working with you off the bed and working on the bed

A passive role – staying in place – is as important as an active role – working with you.

Your dog needs to value the boundary game, e.g. staying on the bed, as much as working with you, for effective turn-taking. Once you have these components, there are some additional bonus games to give it all a boost:

Short-Term Good, Long-Term Better with Boundaries

Play this game with multiple dogs on boundaries where the low value reward is food and the high value reward – which comes when the dogs haven't been rewarded for a longer period – is release to interact and train with you, off the boundary.

"I Choose You!"

Once you have worked on long and short-term rewards with multiple dogs, you can play some fun games where you test and develop the turn-taking skill. This is lots of fun – but not for the faint-hearted or inexperienced dog.

It goes like this:

- Place your dogs on boundaries and then sprint away from them. Return to reward them so they get used to this.

- Once they are good at this, release a single dog as you are running away. The reward for this individual is that he catches up with you – no extra reward is needed or should be given. The reward for the other dogs is that you turn back and feed them.
- Switch dogs regularly, and mix it up by sometimes sprinting off and calling no dog!

This is a great game for developing thinking in arousal, as well as proofing turn-taking.

Name the Boundary

When you have played boundary games with a variety of different 'boundaries', you can begin to give the cue and point to a random area that you have not trained specifically – and your dog will understand. This is so cool; it means that you can give your cue to instigate boundary games (e.g. "hop it up") and point to the area around a lamp post, the shade created by an object, a new object such as tent, chair or sofa, and the criteria that you developed when training boundary games will transfer to this new situation.

CHAPTER 9 UNDERSTANDING AROUSAL

What influences all of the following scenarios?

- Whether your dog can recall while dogs are racing up and down the field.
- Whether he can stop himself from jumping up on you when he has been taught not to.
- The speed with which he reacts to a behaviour you cue.
- The speed with which he runs a course.
- Whether he fulfills the criteria for his contacts or not?
- Whether he is able to perform a behaviour accurately?
- His choice of response when he is presented with something he finds worrying?
- Whether he responds to things in the environment or not?
- Whether he is easy to handle or not?

Any clues? The simple answer is, arousal!

Arousal is a word that is thrown about a lot in dog training circles. It is *the* hot topic for workshops and seminars – and I can guarantee that there will be a ripple of giggles and smirks amongst my students when I start talking about my passion for this topic!

The reason why I feel so passionate about this subject is because I believe that arousal is key for success in so many different areas. Firstly, let's focus on what arousal looks like in dogs and how it presents problems. A dog who is over-aroused may be:

- Reactive to people, other dogs, noises, etc.
- Easily frustrated.
- Cannot cope with failure.
- Will not take rewards.
- Takes his own course.
- Knocks poles.
- Cannot respond to cues.
- Responds slowly or sluggishly.
- Is sticky and hesitant.
- Will not release from a position.
- Releases without cue.

...and I could go on forever with this list!

For better or worse, arousal affects every choice your dog makes, so much so that he may become incapable of making a choice. To understand what is going on, we need to understand what constitutes arousal.

At its basic level arousal refers to your dog's responsiveness; this could be his reaction to events that you instigate (e.g. verbal cues like "sit", 'left") or events he encounters within the environment (e.g. dogs, people, noise). Arousal involves a very complex interaction between the brain (specifically an area called the reticular activating system), and other areas (for example, those involved in hormone production). This affects how likely your dog is to respond to you, and to his environment.

In addition, arousal affects how positive and negative events are processed, and the emotion that results. Therefore, the same event (for example, a dog barking) may result in a completely different emotional and behavioural response, depending on arousal level. This means arousal has both physiological and psychological effects.

The key to companion and performance dog training and behaviour is to understand that arousal is cumulative and doesn't go down quickly. To explain this concept, I use the analogy of an 'arousal bucket'. Small positive or negative triggers of arousal, for example, an agility run or a worrying encounter with a dog, act as additions to the bucket which are being poured in, cup by cup. As water is added to the bucket, and it gets closer to the brim, so the dog gets closer to his threshold of being unable to operate effectively at the level of arousal. Once he gets beyond this threshold, his arousal balance will spill over; excitement is replaced by inefficient over-arousal, worry is replaced with overt fear.

THE AROUSAL BUCKET

Arousal increases step by step (or incident by incident) until it tips over the threshold and the dog can no longer operate effectively.

Further to this, it can take a long time for the bucket to empty, which means that the consequences in terms of emotional upset can be long lasting. When I carried out a study monitoring reactions among a population of pet dogs, many owners noted that their dogs still showed a behavioural response to fireworks or thunder some 72 hours after their initial exposure.

An awareness of this concept is crucial in both companion and performance dog training, as well as working with dogs that are reactive. You need to bear in mind the following:

- Arousal (you may want to think of it as positive and negative stress) is cumulative.
- Both positive and negative events can add to the arousal bucket.
- There is a threshold at which you start to see problems.
- It can take over 72 hours for arousal levels to return to the basal level.

TIME SPAN OF AROUSAL

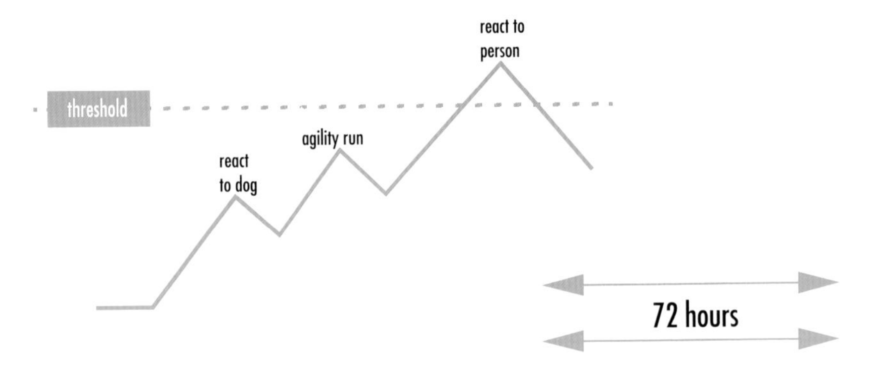

Arousal, regardless of whether it is a negative or a positive experience, has a long lasting effect.

WHAT RESPONSE DO YOU WANT?

One of the biggest misconceptions in dog training is knowing what is the best or most desirable response when a dog is presented with something new or different. This is a matter of significance in a number of situations which include:

- Working with reactive dogs.
- Socialising puppies.
- Assessing rescue dogs before rehoming.
- Assessing service dogs.
- Building trust and confidence in a partnership, regardless of whether it is with a companion dog, a working dog or a performance dog.

To work out the most desirable/appropriate response, take a look at the following scenarios:

A puppy sees a tall gentleman on a walk for the first time and he reacts by:

1. Barking, snarling, trembling.
2. Noticing the man and then orienting back to you and continuing with his walk.
3. Noticing the man, pulling to the end of the lead, and becoming goofy, bouncing around, wiggling and biting on the lead.

An adult, experienced dog sees another leashed dog on a walk and reacts by:

1. Barking, snarling, trembling.
2. Continuing to walk nicely on lead with no change in lead tension (i.e. not beginning to pull, stopping pulling, or changing direction).
3. Noticing the dog, pulling to the end of the lead and becoming keen to interact.

A dog barks and lunges ringside midway through an agility run. Your dog reacts by:

1. Barking, snarling, trembling, changing pace, becoming unresponsive to cues, changing course.
2. Continuing on at same pace, with the same level of responsiveness, not even head turning to look at the dog.
3. Noticing the dog, running to the side of the ring, and then play bowing and barking to prompt interaction.

In each of these scenarios, the most appropriate response is to keep calm and carry on, i.e., showing the minimum change in behaviour – which is option number 2 in each scenario.

My own clinical experience and research suggest that both the overtly 'positive' responses (seemingly wishing to engage) and the overtly 'negative' responses (barking, snarling, trembling) are more likely to lead to reactivity on subsequent occasions compared to the 'neutral' response of carrying on and not changing behaviour. The reason why these overtly positive interactions develop into reactivity can be explained in a number of ways, and is most likely a combination of all of them:

DESIRE BECOMES *FRUSTRATION* BECOMES *FEAR!*

Often the behaviour of a dog that is reactive to other dogs starts in puppyhood with a keen interest in other dogs and a desire for interaction. However, a key piece of learning is missing – other dogs are great but they are not always to be interacted with. As time progresses and the puppy gets larger and less easy to manage in his interactions with other dogs, he is deprived of interacting with every dog as before. The emotion that ensues is frustration, which is evoked when something expected does not occur.

Frustration is a tricky emotion in that, at first, it isn't particularly damaging long-term. However, when repeatedly evoked in relation to other dogs, it increasingly takes the form of fear and anxiety. A negative association has developed as a consequence of the frustration.

THE BUCKET FILLS WITH POSITIVE AND NEGATIVE EVENTS

Regardless of whether events provoke positive or negative stress/arousal, the bucket keeps filling, and therefore contributes to bringing a dog closer to his threshold. The neutral response of being calm, carrying on and being relatively unaffected, has a low arousal associated with it, and the contribution to the fill of the bucket will be much less, safeguarding these dogs from becoming reactive to that particular event in the future.

1. What seems like a 'positive' response could be a coping strategy for anxiety, worry or fear in disguise!

My belief is that a fear response is whatever the dog says it is. The coping strategy he chooses when feeling worried, anxious, scared, frustrated or over-aroused can be anything and everything – and it doesn't always make sense. You only have to think of the abnormal repetitive behaviours of tail chasing, fly catching, self-mutilation or light chasing to appreciate this.

The way a dog chooses to cope with a negative emotion can resemble a positive response to our human eyes; check out the worried dog that opts for going all goofy when he meets dogs, people or the neighbourhood cat.

The behavioural coping strategy a dog adopts may be influenced by:

- The event itself.
- The individual personality of the dog in question.
- What has been effective when coping with similar situations in the past – generally the most commonly used strategy.

Therefore, the safest response in relation to an event is no change in behaviour at all – it is the dog who "keeps calm and carries on". This type, with the desirable, neutral response, does not fall victim to the three roads to reactivity outlined above.

THE AROUSAL BUCKET

Non-reactive and reactive Dogs

This concept is especially important when considering both developing bombproof, non-reactive dogs and working with reactive dogs.

Reactive dogs are often very close to threshold. This may be because they are exposed to numerous small triggers throughout each day in their current routine, e.g. an underlying separation anxiety problem or mild concern about a variety of things. Many behaviourists, trainers and owners perpetuate this by wanting to expose the trigger and "work" with it.

However, the first step in any behaviour case is to ensure we are working with an arousal bucket that is as empty as it can feasibly be. This means providing daily opportunity for the bucket to empty, which means removing stimuli and allowing calm to prevail. There is little point trying to progress emotional and behavioural responses – for example, to dogs on walks – with a bucket that is already three-quarters full because of an inability to settle in the house, barking at the many people who knock on your front door each day, or because of separation anxiety experienced when he is left alone for a four-hour period each day.

Approximately three-quarters of the 'fear of children' cases that I deal with, directly relate to the accumulation of small triggers of anxiety throughout each and every day, over weeks and weeks, leading to a reactivity episode – an overflowing bucket! These dogs often have no, or restricted, opportunity to empty their arousal buckets by being away from the trigger machines (i.e. children), or to implement effective coping strategies in response to the child (e.g. being allowed to leave the room without being followed).

This exact principle applies to non-reactive dogs, too. I am often asked how to stop a problem developing after a first-time experience, such as a dog being attacked, barking at another dog, or lunging at a person. Now the answer is not the thing that we have all done in desperation – chasing every other dog around the park so as to engage in a positive interaction after the attack or the barking episode, or forcing your dog to interact with every bearded gentleman wearing a fluorescent jacket after lunging. The thing to do is *absolutely nothing, and go home!*

It is going to take 72 hours plus before your dog is in a headspace to choose a more appropriate emotional and behavioural response to that situation, let alone learn an alternative to what he has learnt before.

CHAPTER 10
TRAINING FOR CALMNESS

Most dog owner and trainers want their dog to be calm (for at least some of the time) but what is calmness?

In terms of dog training and behaviour, calmness is the emotion that comes about when your dog has low arousal levels and positive things are happening – and that's a pretty nice state to be in...

A CALM DOG IS A HAPPY DOG

If you asked me to describe the perfect existence for a dog, I would say that it would be to live in a state of default calmness. When in doubt, you want your dog to choose calmness as you transition from place to place (whether that be a competition environment, a trip to the park or journey to the vet). But when you want motivation, high arousal and the peak learning and performance head space, you can trigger it.

The good news is that you already have that trigger – it's those behaviours that have been trained with an exciting reinforcement strategy, and it's using those predictors of exciting things (think the words "reeaaaaady" or "hello!"). How cool is that!

A CALM EXISTENCE

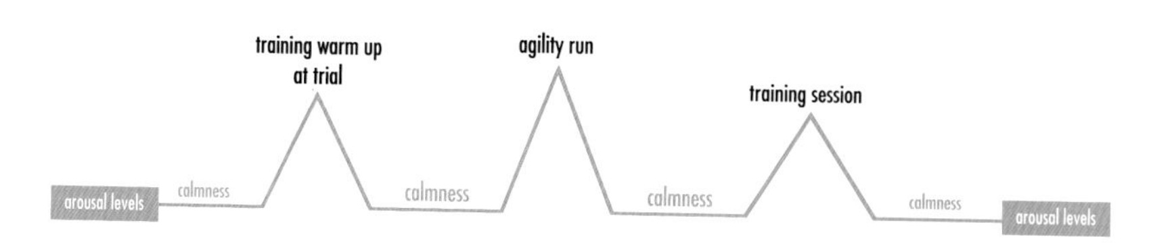

The ideal scenario is for your dog to respond to the triggers of arousal which facilitate learning and performance, but his default is a state of calmness.

The key is that your dog is not only calm but, when there is doubt and you are not giving him direction/cues, he defaults to a calm emotional state and, in turn, chooses behaviours that are associated with that calm state. In other words, his arousal bucket is empty for the majority of the time; he is kept far from the threshold, which enables a consistent level of learning, and allows him to perform to the best of his ability.

MAINTAINING A LEVEL

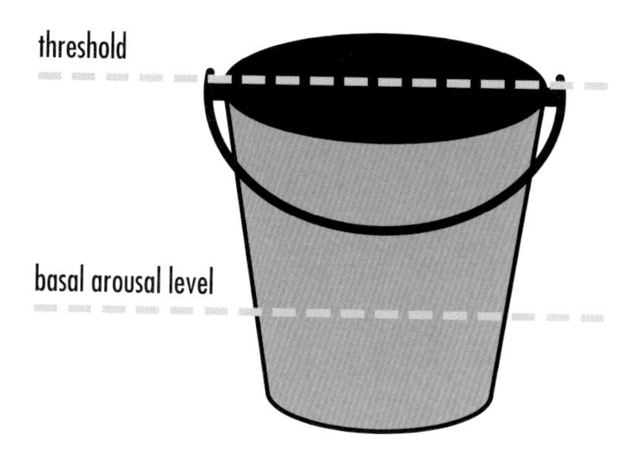

The aim is to maintain the basal – or minimum – level of arousal, thus avoiding the danger of nearing or tipping over the threshold.

A default calm emotional state means that your dog will:

- Conserve his energy, which can then be used for peak learning and performance in training and competition.
- Remain in low arousal and so further from the threshold of over-arousal and fear responses.
- Have a default, positive, emotional state, which will encourage his optimism and his positive choices in novel or ambiguous (potentially scary) situations.
- Spend much of his day in a physiological state adept at recuperating and healing, the so-called parasympathetic nervous system. This healing is vital for companion and sports dogs alike, to prevent injury and allow effective recovery after exercise. Many of the cases with muscular or skeletal injuries that I see in my veterinary work have, in part, come about because of a lack of calmness and low arousal periods throughout the day
- Choose behaviours from the 'calmness behaviour box', such as your dog calmly lying down, sitting at your side, or relaxing with his body stretched out and his head on the floor. Nearly always, these behaviours are more appropriate than the choices that are available in the 'excitement behaviour box' or the 'fear behaviour box'.

So you are sold on developing default calmness in your dog – but how do you get it? I have devised a calmness protocol that has been equally effective when working with severe behaviour cases (from generalised anxiety to repetitive behaviours), and when working with top sports dogs.

CALMNESS PROTOCOL

1. Offer your dog a medium-value treat when he is settled and relaxed. If he gets up from position when you walk away, ignore him. If he stays settled and relaxed, return to him and give him another treat.

- *Do not use a clicker or any other excitable marker for this – silence is most effective! Give the treat calmly and deliberately.*
- *Do not be disheartened if your dog gets up or becomes excited after delivering the reward, the calm behaviour is what has been reinforced.*

Initially, if your dog gets up or becomes excited as you walk towards him with the treat, you can still give it to him. However, once your dog knows the game, only reward when he doesn't move and doesn't get excited.

- *In complex, especially distracting or dangerous environments, you will increase success if your dog is on lead to begin with. The best plan is to start working an easy location and then increase the difficulty.*
- *Make sure you reward your dog when his body is relaxed and he is not focusing on the food – don't create a 'calmness faker!'*

2. Ignore your dog – especially when he is opting for attention-seeking behaviours. Wait for the moment he settles and relaxes and then call him over to you for attention. Do not do this too regularly or he may start to yoyo between his floor space and where you are located. However, this strategy is a great way to communicate to your dog that the attention-seeking behaviours won't work – but being calm, relaxed and relatively independent will!
3. Time the rewards (treat or attention) with external distractions. For example, wait until someone is walking past the house, you hear a dog barking in the distance, or when someone starts cheering in the neighbouring agility ring. This rewards your dog for remaining calm in the face of distraction. In addition, it changes his emotional response from being negative (beings anxious or over-aroused in the face of distractions) to being positive (reacting to external distractions with calmness/low arousal).

TOP TIP!

When you are faced with challenging situation, use a reward dispenser – a toy containing treats, such as a kong or a dried hoof – as a long-lasting reinforcement. Working to get the treats, or chewing on the hoof will further promote calmness and relaxation. This is especially useful when you cannot give your full attention, but you want to keep on rewarding calmness. Suitable fillings might include meat or coconut oil.

Start by working on this protocol in your home, but then take it on the road. Try it out in at least six different environments to aid the generalisation of this default emotional state. Couple this with additional tools, especially on and off switch behaviours (see page 151) and boundary games (see page 100) – and enjoy the results!

If you follow the calmness protocol as described above, you will have the means of creating a well-behaved and calm dog who is in a positive emotional state and therefore has the ability to learn and perform at the peak of his potential.

The calmness protocol in combination with crated/boundary rest and passive calming activities, such as chewing and treat dispenser play, make up the approach that I use for all dogs to achieve the ideal scenario of an empty bucket.

When you account for these three elements in your dog – each of which has a varying level of choice and difficulty – you can transition any dog from manic to calm in any household and any environment. Calmness protocol involves the most choice in this framework; the dog is free to choose what he does and where he goes to a certain extent.

The rest component involves less choice, with the dog being in a crate or on a boundary or raised bed (if he is experienced at boundary games). I am often asked why this element is so beneficial and crucial. Here's the thing: choice is tiring. You

CALMNESS DEVELOPMENT WHEEL

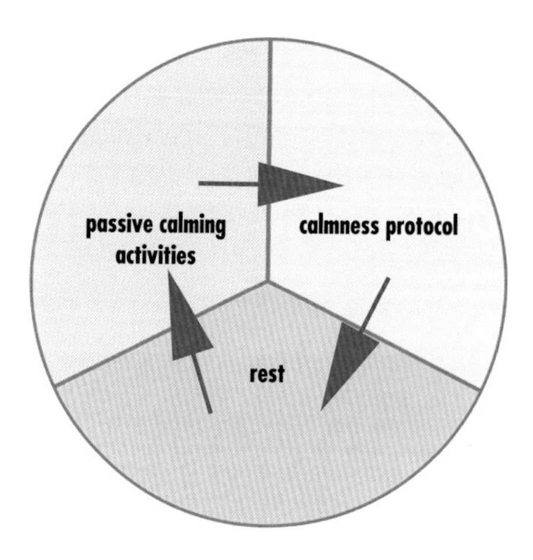

Calmness is rarely a natural state of mind – it has to be learnt and encouraged.

therefore need to incorporate and develop parts of your dog's routine where he doesn't have to choose, where he doesn't have the pressure of expectation from you, and where he is shielded from the busy environment he lives in.

Passive, calming activities are an interim between the two previous activities. Your dog is free to do what he wants but there is a clear choice for him to make, for example engage with the filled kong, search for scattered food in the garden, or chew on a meaty bone. Rotating your dog around these three activities is not only a comprehensive approach to developing calmness, it also becomes a way of life. It is a way of managing your dog in a complex and changing world and enhancing his personality to suit all the jobs that he is required to do.

Every dog has his own arousal level which is part of his unique personality. Developing this default, basal arousal level towards calmness is one the most valuable things you could ever teach your dog!

MULTI-DOG HOUSEHOLDS AND CALMNESS TRAINING

Managing a multi-dog household is a challenge – and achieving calmness in this environment can appear to be well nigh impossible. But it doesn't have to be this way!

In multi dog households, I believe that calmness should prevail for 95 per cent of the time; the remaining 5 per cent being allocated to training and other scheduled activities. The fundamental reason for problems that arise in multi-dog households, relating to both training and behaviour, is a failure to reach an acceptable level of calmness – resulting in a very full arousal bucket. This may cause problems within the home, such as inter-dog fights, reactivity when out and about, or lack of focus, reliability, impulse control or motivation in the sports arena.

When first beginning to develop calmness in a multi-dog household, the key is to work with one dog at a time, focusing on each of the three tridents of the calmness development wheel (see page 119).

For example, I might work on the calmness protocol with Illy, my Standard Poodle, while Betcha, my young Border Collie, is engaging in a passive calming activity with a filled kong, and a friend's dog, who is staying with me, may be relaxing in a crate. I would then rotate them around – Betcha doing the calmness protocol, my friend's dog enjoying a chew, and Illy resting on a raised bed.

This approach is important for three reasons:

1. It allows you to concentrate on the training part – the calmness protocol – where your observation skills are needed to ensure you are rewarding the right behaviours and attitude within the behaviour. Working with all your dogs on calmness protocol at the same time, right away – without first working with them individually – will probably make you frantic, and therefore less able to

CALMING ACTIVITIES IN A MULTI-DOG HOUSEHOLD

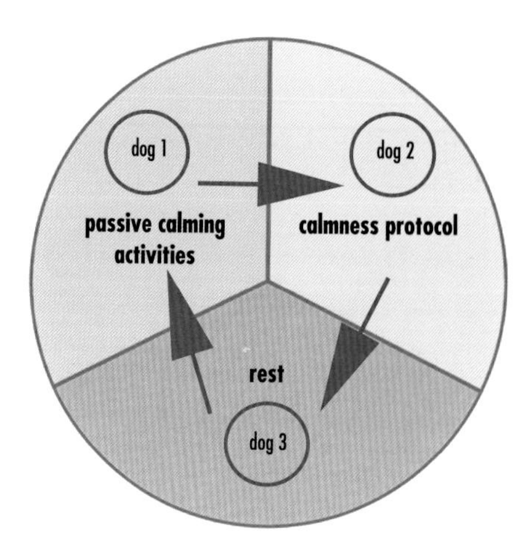

Activities can be rotated among dogs to create a calm environment.

reward the behaviour you want to see.

2. It makes the dog's job of the calmness protocol a whole lot easier as the choice to lie down in a calm manner, settle and ignore distractions is so much more likely to happen when everyone else is doing the same thing, being employed in passive calming activities, and resting on boundaries.
3. It gives the dogs variety in their calmness training, which improves their success rate and is more manageable and flexible in day-to-day living. It becomes a way of life and is especially useful when you own more than three dogs.

CHAPTER 11
AROUSAL – THE GOOD, THE BAD, THE UGLY

We have discussed the dangers of over-arousal in dogs, but the presence of arousal is also a vital ingredient in dog training, especially for the sports dog.

THE GOOD...

The right level of arousal builds intensity into behaviours. In dog sports, this leads to confidence, consistency, precision and speed – fundamental characteristics for the successful

THE OPTIMUM AROUSAL LEVEL

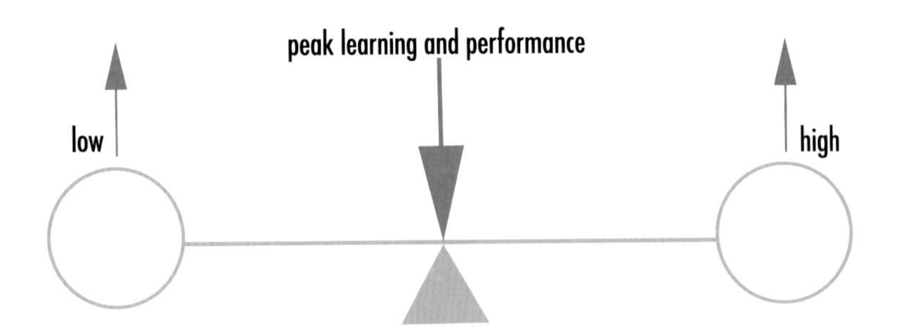

A dog will perform to the best of his ability when he is at the optimum arousal level.

performance dog. I refer to this optimum arousal level as the point of peak learning and performance. Whether in training or in competition, it creates that ideal level of responsiveness and excitement so the right choice is more likely to be made.

Further to this, the choice is made quickly, without doubt and, in turn, without worry or conflict of emotion. This level of learning and performance is a product of a super reinforcement history for the right choices *and* optimum arousal level. Neither optimum arousal level without a reinforcement history for the right choice, nor a reinforcement history without optimum arousal level will result in perfect performance.

Arousal is an inevitable component of the environments we use for training and competing – and it will always be there! Therefore the ability to balance arousal, and to be able to think in arousal, is crucial to success.

In summary, we need arousal. Without it, we would have flat, slow and imprecise companion and sports dogs. What's more, we don't only need it – we can't avoid it! We expect our sports dogs to learn and perform in highly arousing environments, so it is vital that we take on board the effects of arousal and understand how to work with it. Whether your dog reaches high arousal in your training sessions or not, every dog is inevitably going to meet it at some point in their lives and it is our job to prepare them for it.

THE BAD...

Too much arousal is the most common problem I see in my behaviour consultations and in my sports coaching. In the past, sports training was all about upping arousal levels. But we now know that continuing to increase arousal is detrimental and damaging to both learning and performance!

This phenomenon in animals was first described by Yerkes & Dodson in 1908 following a study where (rightly or wrongly) they applied electric shocks to rats that were being tasked to complete a maze. They found that application of shocks

THE RISK OF OVER AROUSAL

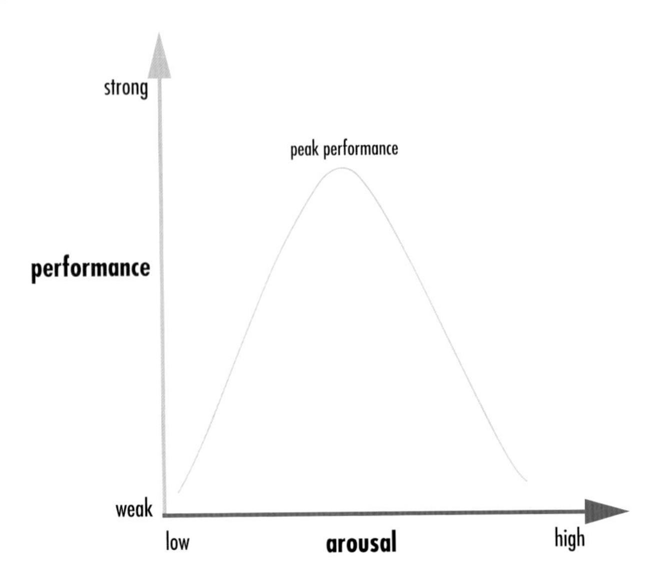

If the optimum arousal level is exceeded, performance level will drop off.

increased performance and therefore concluded that increased levels of arousal/stress had a positive effect on performance. However, they also discovered that at a certain point beyond peak performance, increasing arousal levels were detrimental to performance of the task. This became known as the Yerkes-Dodson Law and it is a very useful construct in dog training.

MAKING CHOICES

Let's return to our analogy of tunnels and the way a dog's choice of tunnel is influenced by how reinforced (or luxurious it is), based on his knowledge of what has happened in the past. From this perspective, arousal beyond the optimum level makes a dog less selective about his tunnel choices. He no longer cares about receiving champagne on arrival in his chosen tunnel; he no longer cares if the carpets are nicer in the 'impulse control tunnel' compared to the 'charge around barking and ignoring you tunnel'. This has two important consequences:

1. The tunnels you have repeatedly reinforced – those you want to show off in training class or in competition – are no longer important to your dog. The tunnels you don't want your dog to use: the 'rampaging around the class tunnel', the 'I'm going to do my own course tunnel', the 'barking tunnel' are now worth considering. As far as your dog is concerned, the currency you were working with has lost its value; he is no longer using it when he is making his choices.

2. Suddenly, every tunnel becomes a possibility. Reinforcement history has vanished! Your dog is presented with thousands of tunnels for every given situation, and he can't decide what to do! What does a dog do when he can't make up his mind?

You might find that your dog stares at you, lip licks, looks as though 'the lights are on but nobody is home'. He might be unable to respond to any of his learnt cued behaviours.

Alternatively, he might do everything in slow motion, moving sluggishly and stickily. Why? Because for every second that he is performing the behaviour, he is being re-presented with thousands of choices to work through. Think about it: there are too many tunnels and too little time, so he freezes or goes into slow-mo!

I look at arousal levels in dogs as a spectrum where increasing arousal may move a dog from under-arousal through to higher arousal and finally to over-arousal. At some point in this journey of increasing arousal, he will hit the optimum arousal level where he exhibits peak learning and performance. This is the point you want to reach when training and competing with your dog but, first and foremost, you need to avoid under arousal and over-arousal!

THE AROUSAL JOURNEY

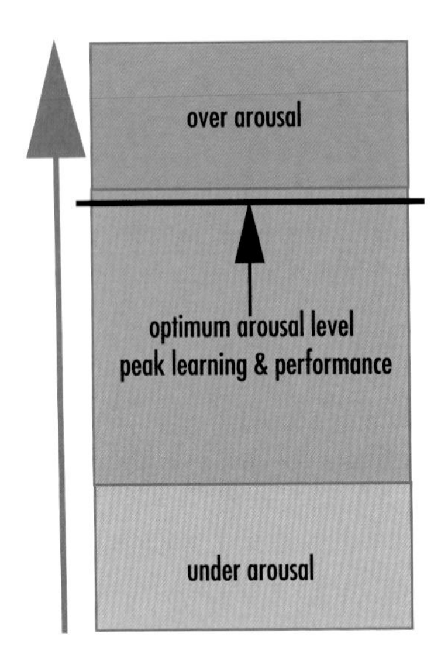

A dog will travel from low to high arousal – and on that journey he will hit the optimum arousal level.

AROUSAL IS JOB-SPECIFIC

Unfortunately finding the optimum level of arousal, thereby avoiding under arousal and over-arousal, is not as simple as it sounds. This is because there are specific areas of learning and specific behaviours that lend themselves to a certain level of arousal.

A general rule that is used in human psychology (summarised very nicely by human psychologist, Nicky Hayes below) is that simpler tasks are more tolerant of higher arousal levels and are less susceptible to decreased performance when arousal increases.

She states:

"The optimal level of arousal varies for different tasks, with complex tasks showing an earlier performance decrement than

TASK SPECIFIC

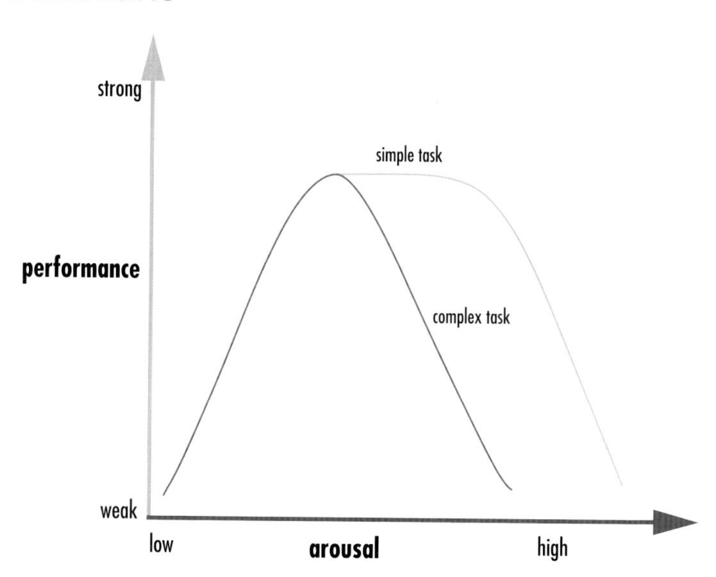

Simple tasks are more tolerant of arousal levels so performance is less likely to drop off.

simple tasks, for the same level of arousal. In other words, if we are performing a relatively simple task, then we can cope with a much larger range of arousal levels – the curve is flatter. So, for example, if you are doing the washing-up, you would not do it very well if your state of arousal was very low indeed, and you were half-asleep; but equally, you would be very upset indeed if you started to break things (accidentally, that is).

"But if you were engaged in a complex task, like trying to write an essay, you might need to be a bit more aroused – or at least, alert – before you could get started. Equally, however, getting upset would interfere with your ability to write the essay much more than it would interfere with your ability to wash up."

(Hayes, 2000)

TAILORING AROUSAL TO THE TASK

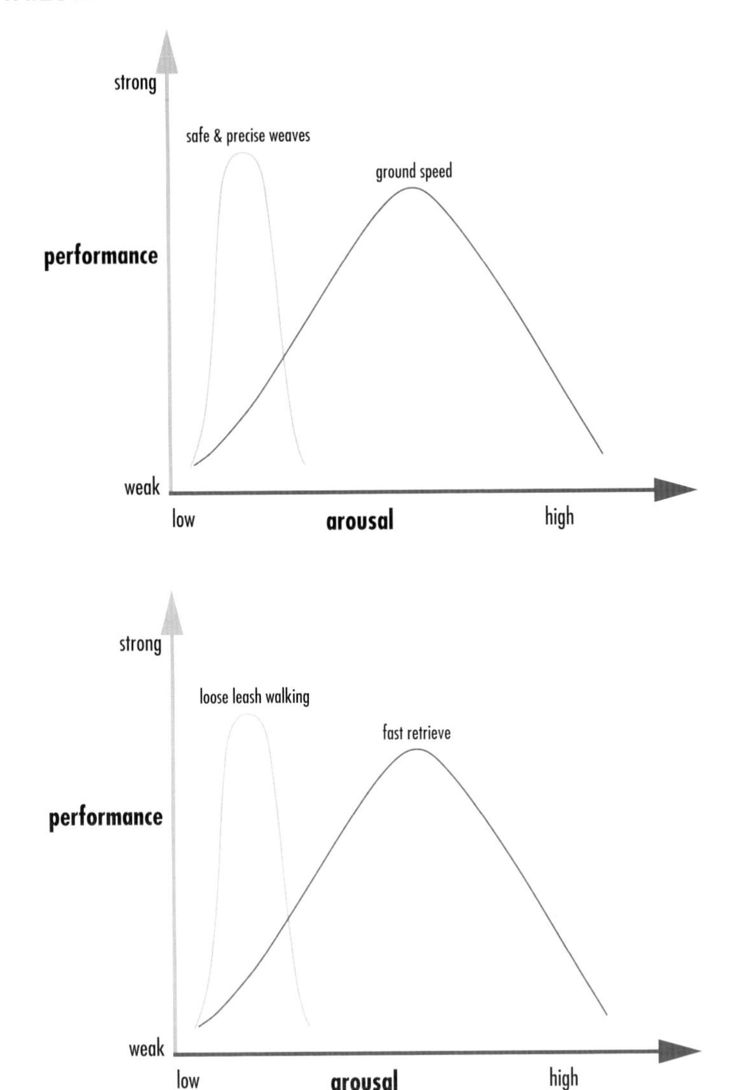

A complex task, such as learning to weave, or maintaining the correct heelwork position, is best attempted when arousal levels are low. High-intensity, or endurance tasks, such as covering the ground at speed, or carrying out a fast retrieve, are best learnt and performed with a higher level of arousal.

Further to this, the learner benefits from much lower arousal when learning and performing challenging tasks that involve a lot of discrimination (a lot of tunnels to choose from) and/or precision. A good example of this would be a dog learning the heel position or being taught to go through the weaves. Conversely, tasks where intensity or endurance is the name of the game – and options are relatively reduced – benefit naturally from higher arousal levels in both learning acquisition and performance.

THE CHALLENGE OF SPORT

This is where it gets challenging for those of us that train and compete in sports – and this applies to every sport. Dog sports are made up of a chain of behaviours, each with a different optimum arousal level and tolerance to arousal levels – and it's done that way on purpose! It is fundamentally what makes training, competing and watching dog sports so captivating.

In agility, there is nothing more inspiring than watching a dog switch from flat out running, to swimming through the weaves, to stopping dead on the bottom of a seesaw, and then measuring his pace for a turn. Equally, in obedience, we marvel when we see a dog moving from snappy position transitions, to precise and close heelwork, and switching from duration to movement so effortlessly. It captures our hearts.

These sequences of behaviours have very different ideal arousal levels (as illustrated in the diagram to the left). In this scenario *Behaviour A* (safe and fast weaves) is compared to *Behaviour B* (groundspeed).

Behaviour A is clearly less tolerant of higher arousal levels, with performance dropping off as arousal increases. In the case of the weaves, reduced performance may not be simply refusing to weave or leaving the weaves early, but rather changes in the speed, the fluidity or the precision and safety of the action.

Behaviour B, on the other hand, clearly benefits from the

higher arousal; performance does not really increase or reach its peak until a much higher arousal level is attained, compared to *Behaviour A*. Behaviours that follow this pattern may be flat out running in agility, left and right spin tricks or a sendaway in obedience.

Imaging and considering the expected arousal curve in a behaviour you are planning to train, or have already trained, can really help in fine-tuning and achieving perfect performance.

We have to prepare our dogs for this, and to be truly competitive we cannot sacrifice the performance of the higher arousal behaviour – for example, groundspeed – at the expense of the lower arousal behaviour – for example, the weaves. We therefore need to build the tolerance of the lower arousal behaviour to higher arousal. This is something termed ‘thinking in arousal’ and is a concept we need to develop in its own right.

CHAPTER 12
THINKING IN AROUSAL

Thinking in arousal is a concept that is both universal and behaviour-specific. It is crucial to success in both companion and sports dog training.

Struggles that might suggest a lack of aptitude in thinking in arousal would be:

- Recalls are focused at home and in the park – but not at the training class or any variation on this.
- Results do not transfer to competition nor translate to competition results.
- Inability to learn behaviours involving precision/accuracy.
- Inability to perform the behaviour in the presence of a particular reward, e.g. the opportunity to chase a tennis ball, greet other dogs, etc.
- Loss of reliability, precision or criteria in behaviours with increased excitement.

Developing thinking in arousal has the following benefits:

- It makes the arousal-performance curves of your dog's learnt behaviours wider and flatter so they can better be performed in higher arousal.
- It develops your dog's ability to think and learn effectively in higher arousal.

TEACHING TOLERANCE TO AROUSAL

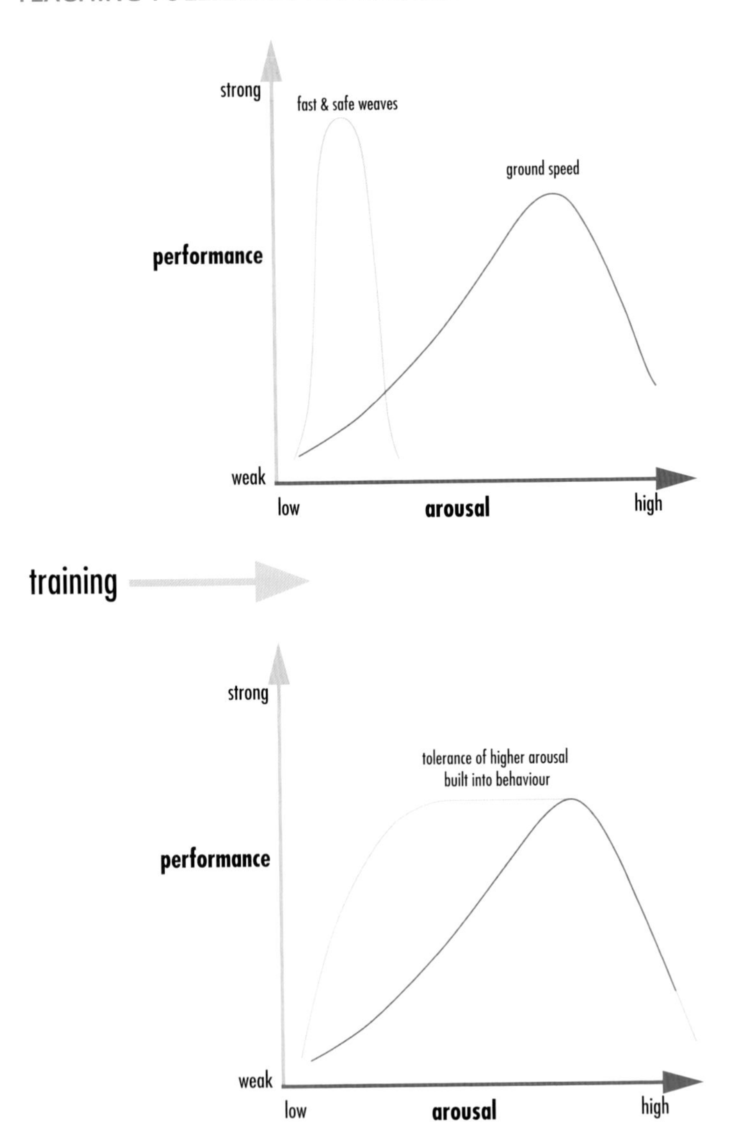

A dog who is able to process information when in a state of arousal will perform his task more effectively and will produce more consistent results.

GAMES TO PLAY

There are a number of games you can play to promote thinking in arousal.

Run and Cue

- Start playing this game on lead. While loose-lead walking at a reasonable pace, ask for a behaviour your dog knows on cue and reward him by running ahead with him.
- Repeat this and see his focus and arousal increase. The faster you up the pace, the higher the arousal, and the more your dog will have to think through arousal.

It's a great game and, as a much appreciated side effect, it creates really focused loose-lead walking, too!

RUN AND CUE

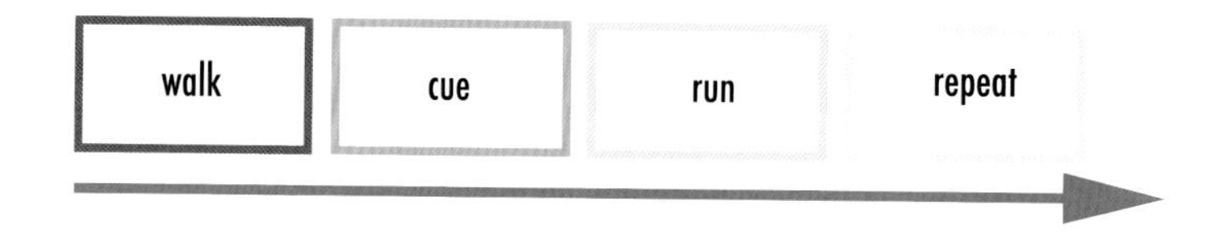

Ask your dog to repeat a learnt behaviour as you increase his arousal level by introducing speed.

Orientation and Cues

I play this game to build intensity and reliability in my obedience transitions. It's one of the ways I get the snappy transitions that you may have seen in dogs I have trained.

- Start by throwing a piece of food out and reward your dog for orienting back to you by throwing another piece of food out.
- Create a little food circuit, from side to side, so that you dog is running in front of you.

- Periodically, ask for a cued behaviour before throwing the next piece of food.
- Reward correct performance of the cued behaviour by throwing the food out, and continuing the bouncing back and forth.

In order to create the most effective thinking in arousal, keep the game unpredictable by mixing the cues you give and the order you give them, and make sure that most of the time, your dog is simply chasing the food back and forth.

ORIENTATION AND CUES

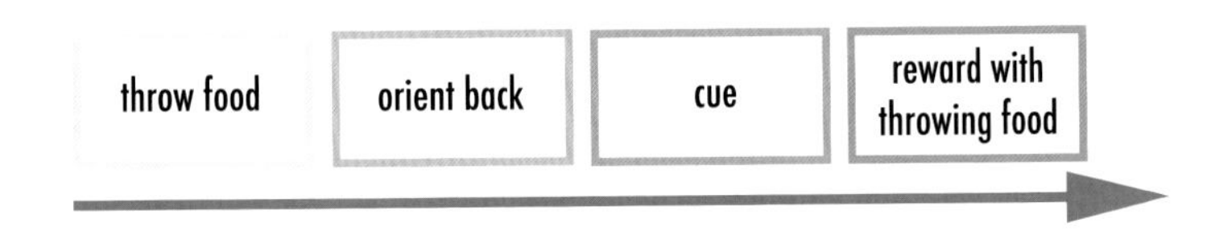

This game asks a dog to think in the midst of the excitement of food being thrown for him.

Advanced orientation and cues

You can increase the degree of difficulty by changing the order. Throw the food out, ask for a behaviour and then release to the food.

ADVANCED ORIENTATION AND CUES

Increase the difficulty by adding an "ok go" as a release to get the food.

Whip It!

This game teaches a number of valuable concepts which include:

- Impulse control.
- Thinking in arousal.
- Tolerance of frustration.
- Susceptibility to reinforcement.
- Movement.

All you need is a reasonably open space (the smaller the dog, the smaller the space required), a horse lunge whip, and a fluffy toy to attach to the whip, or you can buy a purpose-made flirt pole. There are three stages to the game; it is absolutely crucial that the steps are followed in order and that you do not progress from one step to the next until the behaviour is fully established. Rushing through the stages can compromise the valuable concepts that you are teaching.

Step 1: Chase

This is the most important step:

- Animate the toy on the end of the lunge whip and get your dog chasing it along the ground. Keep the lunge whip low and ahead of your dog.
- For very fast dogs, it is easier to keep a step ahead by rotating your entire body so that your dog periodically circles your body. Occasionally he will succeed in grabbing the toy. Try to establish a nice balance between chasing and grabbing the toy in order to keep motivation high and to maintain intensity in the pursuit.
- When your dog grabs the toy, don't ask him to drop it or release it. But when he lets go to re-grip, simply whip it away from him. This builds even more desire for chasing and catching.
- Keep sessions very short and high in energy.

We need this game to emulate all exciting impulses your dog experiences in everyday life, so it is essential to keep it free flowing. If you add rules too early, or apply too much pressure, your dog will not be able to learn the valuable concepts that are embedded within the game. The game may inadvertently become something detached from real-life impulses and be perceived simply as a trick.

Step 2: Control

This is where you ask your dog to control himself – and it is really important that you don't attempt this too early. You want the chase to represent every highly distracting, highly exciting event in his life. If you add control too early – before you have created the ravenous, crazy desire for the toy – you will never get the result you want.

- Now, when your dog is chasing, flip the toy from side to side until he stops still and waits. The instant he shows self-control, reward him with his release word ("ok go") and activate the toy again.
- It is crucial that you balance the first two steps of this game – chase and control. Over-doing the control step will ruin the behaviour, and concepts, you are training long-term. Typically, a ratio of ten chasing repetitions to one control is adequate, but some very diligent dogs may need more repetitions of chase to keep the game true to its purpose.

Step 3: Operate

This step builds thinking in arousal in your dog – and it is the really fun bit!

- When your dog is stood still, exhibiting self-control, ask for a behaviour that he knows very well, on cue. The first behaviour you cue is important: it should not be your dog's default/favourite behaviour, but he should be totally reliable when asked to perform it. For example, a Border Collie will naturally default to a down, so I would choose another behaviour, e.g. a sit or left spin, for the purposes of this game. Equally, a Springer Spaniel may naturally default to a sit so, in this case, I would use a down.

- Keep everything very fast-paced and release your dog to chase as soon as he has completed the cued behaviour. Keep him guessing and mix up the cues you give, making sure to keep balance with repetitions of chase, chase, chase!
- Finally, ask your dog for a chain of behaviours before being released, for example sit, stand, left, "ok go!".

Bonus Whip It Games

Recall and run: Can your dog recall from the whip to be sent back to it?

Middle and run: Can you recall your dog to "middle" (sat between your legs, see page 154) and send him back to chase?

Wrap and run: Can your dog wrap around a wing, tree or barrel before being released to the chase?

Sport and run: Can you send your dog to perform an agility obstacle, or some obedience heelwork, and then send to the whip?

"OK Go" With Other High-Arousal Events

This game works on the same principle as the whip it game (see above), and combines it with the "ok go" game (see page 86).

- Start using the "ok go" cue for really highly exciting events. For example, to allow your dog to:
  - race other dogs
  - go into an agility tunnel
  - swim in the sea
  - sniff
  - greet people
  - greet other dogs
  - anything that your dog absolutely loves!

- This time, wait for impulse control (for example, eye contact, a control position such as sit or down, before giving the "ok go" cue. Make sure you balance this with step one – sending him straight to the distraction without waiting for impulse control – to maintain high value for the fun behaviour itself.
- As for the whip it game, you can then ask for a behaviour before giving the "ok go" cue.

TAKE IT TO THE START-LINE

Playing the "ok go" game with behaviours on the start-line is a great way to build thinking in arousal into your agility training and competing.

To recap, arousal affects how responsive your dog is to events occurring from you (e.g. cues) and the environment (e.g. other dogs, people, etc.). Arousal has both psychological and physiological effects; it can be a good thing or a bad thing, and, in turn, there is an optimum arousal level where your dog exhibits peak learning and performance. This optimum arousal level lies on the arousal spectrum below over-arousal and above under-arousal. We can make behaviours more tolerant of arousal by developing the concept of thinking in arousal.

To be able to achieve optimum arousal level, you need to get a feel for what over-arousal might look like, in order to avoid it. Over-arousal can look very different for different dogs; it may be mistaken for other things or it may not be identified at all. I see a lot of behaviour cases where the dog presents with lunging, barking, screaming, sometimes biting people and other dogs, and sometimes even his owner. This picture of reactivity certainly looks as though it is triggered by a fear response. But after delving into the dog's history, over-arousal is often the single cause or, at least, a contributing factor.

Quite simply, over-arousal is the level of arousal at which your dog no longer operates properly – his learning and performance is impaired by the high-arousal. However, there are plenty of indicators, clues and signals that tell you he is approaching his threshold; the arousal bucket is filling and is danger of spilling over! See the table below for some of the many presenting clues of over-arousal or approaching over-arousal.

CLUES OF OVER-AROUSAL

examples of the clues of over-arousal		
barking	howling	growling
hiding	escaping	pulling on lead
lagging on lead	chasing	trembling/shaking
being restless	pacing	being vigilant
circling	seeking out people	increasing owner attachment
salivating	lip licking	panting
a stronger/harder mouth when taking treats	cheek puffing	yawning
staring	ground sniffing	self grooming
scratching	any form of aggression	lead lunging
biting lead	playing, aggressing or staring at invisible things	unresponsiveness
freezing	important disinterest in treats that are normally enjoyed	important inability to respond to learnt cues

This list shows the huge number of different ways that over-arousal can present – and this list is by no means exhaustive. It is, therefore, crucial to be able to appreciate and identify behaviours that are associated with over-arousal in your own

READING THE CLUES

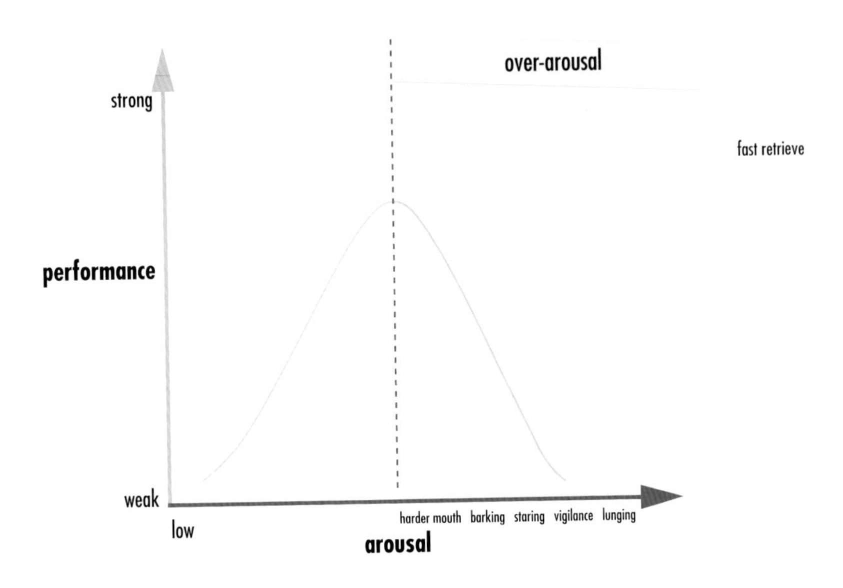

Monitor your dog to track when he is becoming over-aroused.

dog, especially if you are competing with him. It's about becoming an expert on your dog's behaviour!

Once you are aware of how over-arousal looks, you can then get a feel for how optimum arousal level looks. This is where the understanding becomes very powerful. Remember optimum arousal level is the point at which your dog attains peak learning and performance. How useful would it be to achieve this arousal level in a training environment or on the start-line? Incredibly so!

HOW TO IDENTIFY THE OPTIMUM AROUSAL LEVEL

Well, this is the time in training or in competition that just feels awesome. Your dog achieves that balance between snappy speed and perfect precision, and it fills you with pride. It is the way in which special behaviours are performed that most accurately indicate whether optimum arousal level has been achieved. These behaviours can become your optimum arousal indicators and will be a vital part of your toolbox!

They include:

- A down behaviour that is quick and performed without hesitation when a reinforcer (food or toy) is placed out ahead on the floor.
- Following completion of a cued behavior, no further behaviours are offered.
- Performing a pop-up sit from a down position, without getting out of position.
- Executing a stand from sit, with front paws staying in position.
- Performing a sit pretty when cued (this one is a great test on the start-line).
- Heeling without over-rotation on left turns (for obedience fanatics!).

Learn what behaviours start to look like when your dog goes above the optimum arousal level:

- A sloppy sit
- Offering behaviours without cues.
- Creeping forward when being asked for a wait.
- A sluggish left spin.
- A wobbly sit pretty.

Then learn what behaviours look like when he is under the optimum arousal level:

- Offering a behaviour that requires less energy investment than the one you asked for, e.g. a sit instead of a down.
- Losing eye contact.
- Wondering off.
- Losing speed in behaviours.

This learning will enable you to pick up the clues that will identify that sought after optimum level, which allows your dog to learn and perform to the very best of his ability.

CHAPTER 13 MANIPULATING AROUSAL

Arousal is intensely powerful in dogs; the ability to influence and manipulate it is crucial to success in:

- Achieving optimum learning and performance from your companion or sports dog.
- Creating a dog that is able to calm down after exciting or scary events.
- Working effectively with a reactive dog and ensuring no reactivity episodes occur.

To be able to achieve and maintain optimum arousal levels and, equally, to avoid arousal and over-arousal in situations where we do not want it, we must learn how to manipulate arousal levels. There are a number of tools at your disposal in any situation when aiming to change the arousal levels of your dog.

1. REINFORCEMENT AND AROUSAL

This is a good tool to start with, as you have it already: it's the reinforcement strategy. Remember that to reinforce a behaviour is to strengthen and enhance that tunnel (or pathway) in your dog's brain so that it is more likely to be used in the future.

So the tunnel with air conditioning, nice lighting and appealing flooring (maybe a recall) is selected over a dark and dingy tunnel with fewer enhancements (maybe chase the squirrel across the field). In addition, the way you reinforce your dog will influence arousal levels associated with:

- That specific training situation.
- Future situations when that behaviour will be cued (i.e. that tunnel is used).

Arousal becomes intrinsic to the behaviour so your dog's arousal levels will be increased or decreased accordingly whenever that behaviour is cued. This means that you need to consciously consider arousal when you are selecting a reinforcement strategy, and decide what the end goal for arousal is before you reward a behaviour.

The logic of this becomes clear if you take an extreme example, such as rewarding a reactive dog for ignoring another dog by creating a very high arousal orient to you on cue (a game of tug, for example). This will inject arousal into a situation already dominated by anxiety and will, quite easily, create a reactivity episode. In contrast, a low arousal cue such as "watch" is more likely to generate a calm reaction.

It is often thought that consistency and reliability is only possible in high arousal behaviours. However, calm behaviours can be equally as consistent and reliable. Therefore, the decision as to whether a behaviour should be high or low arousal should be decided based on its future purpose – in other words, the situations that behaviour is needed for and the characteristics of that behaviour.

Reinforcement strategy, specifically the reinforcer itself and the delivery of that reinforcer, can increase or decrease arousal, the degree of which may also be dependent on the individual dog. Therefore, you need to consider what effect different reinforcers and deliveries have on your dog. For example, most dogs find food is calming compared to other reinforcers, but

REINFORCEMENT STRATEGY

arousal level:	low arousal/calm	high arousal/intense
Example reinforcement strategy choices:	Reinforcers: kibble, long-lasting chews, stroking access to sniffing, etc. Delivery: Calm placement to mouth, on floor, cupping, calm verbal release etc.	Reinforcers: tug toy, tennis ball, flirt pole, liver cake, frisbee, access to play with another dog etc. Delivery: throwing, catching, chasing, tugging, rolling, exciting verbal release etc.
Tunnel enhancements:	Comfy sofas, rugs, a warm fire, a harpist, candles and aromatherapy, canine massage therapists etc.	Strobe lighting, smoke machine, disc jockey, light-up flooring etc.

Consider the effect different reinforcers will have on your dog's behaviour.

for a small number of dogs it can have the opposite effect – it sends them sky high!

To clarify, I have included a table of reinforcement strategy choices and their possible consequences on arousal for my dog, Betcha (above).

Now that we know how to reinforce to increase and decrease arousal, the next step is to consider what to reinforce. This is significant because what you reinforce influences the arousal level of a situation just as much as how you reinforce it. I view this as the difference between movement and duration.

Movement

Where you reward movement (so your dog is moving rather than when he has finished a behaviour), a number of things happen:

- Arousal levels increase.
- Further movement is promote…therefore increasing arousal further.

Pairing this with an arousal-increasing reinforcement strategy, such as throwing a tennis ball or throwing food out, promotes further arousal and also keeps the dog moving. This is a powerful formula for developing arousal and increasing motivation when it is required.

Duration

On the flipside, rewarding duration – the maintenance of behaviours or static positions – will decrease arousal. This is a great way of calming dogs that have become over-aroused, for example, frequent feeding for continuing to maintain a sit or down position. Pairing this with a calming reinforcement strategy – bringing the food to your dog's mouth slowly, or cupping it on the floor, and only giving it when he is calm, is a powerful way of giving a reward and lowering arousal.

Learning Through Play!

- Devise a training session of position behaviours (sit, down, stand, bow, sit pretty, you name it!) where you mark your dog for movement only. For example, instead of marking the maintenance of a sit, mark him as he moves to adopt the sit, and as he moves out of position after a release.
- Now plan a training session where you do the exact opposite: reward your dog only when he is stationary in the behaviour. Note how the arousal levels of each session are poles apart!

Of course, life, training and competing are far more complex than utilising a simple *on* or *off* switch. It is a continuing awareness of your dog's arousal levels – where you want them to be and where you don't want them to be – that makes the difference between disaster and success.

This means that as you become more skilled at assessing and responding to what your dog is telling you, you will be able to adapt to the situation in front of you. On a minute-by-minute basis, this will give you the opportunity to manipulate *how* and *what* you reinforce to get the results that you want.

2. GAMES AND AROUSAL

Playing games are key in manipulating arousal – and they are also lots of fun! I work with a couple of games that I have found to be effective with virtually all performance and behaviour problems that are related to arousal levels.

This could range from a dog that is knocking poles, to a dog that is lunging towards everything in sight. These games embrace the concept of rewarding movement to increase arousal and rewarding duration to decrease arousal – and both are equally important in upping the fun and success!

Reward Nothing Game

This involves rewarding your dog, using a low arousal reward and delivery choice, for doing – you guessed it – absolutely nothing!

This is what you do:

- Prepare 10 treats.
- Sit down in front of your dog.
- Watch closely, and every time you see him pause for a second, relax or take a breath – reward him!
- Wait until he stills again, then reward.

The only two rules in this game are:

1. Your dog is still when you deliver the reward.
2. You can only deliver the reward if he maintains 'doing nothing' as you bring the reward to him.

Your dog can adopt any position he chooses; the key is that

for the course of the session, he is doing absolutely nothing when you deliver each of the 10 treats. The aim is to capture that moment of bringing the energy down, switching off and relaxing the muscles.

This is a powerful game; it builds value in lower arousal, builds value in doing nothing and creates a dog that is likely to have lower arousal in the future. It is also a great game for those situations when you need to return to a low arousal headspace. So, for example if your dog has reacted to seeing another dog, you can help him to transition from high arousal to lower arousal.

It is ideal for dogs who are:

- Easily aroused.
- Easily frustrated.
- Lack impulse control in high arousal.
- Anxious, especially in different environments.

It is useful in the following situations:

- As an environmental warm-up for dogs that may be reactive or lacking confidence.
- To transition to a thinking, lower arousal state of mind after an episode of over-arousal, frustration or reactivity.
- To restore a state of low arousal after allowing high arousal, for example after an agility run!

This game tips the arousal balance to facilitate a calmer state of mind and, in high-risk situations, it can be used to bring a dog to lower arousal, thus protecting his emotional state. Remember, a calm dog is a happy dog!

This is an extremely valuable game to take on the road and practise in lots of different environments. Try it out while sitting on a bench in the park, mid training class, in competition environments, and in the vet's waiting room.

Predictability increases arousal; that is why all the above

situations become very high arousal (positive: excitement or negative: fear) as we are very predictable with them. We always do something exciting at training class or in a competition arena; for some dogs, the vet's waiting room is a place of fear. Calmness and 'doing nothing' is never naturally associated with these environments in day-to-day life due to their nature.

However, by playing 'reward nothing' we not only get the arousal lowering benefits of the game, we also reduce the predictability and therefore stop over-arousal in these situations in the future.

Reward Anything Game

Now, let's consider the flipside of this game – you've guessed it, the reward anything game!

I use this game for a dog that:

- Needs more motivation.
- Needs more arousal.
- Is new to shaping.
- Lacks confidence in offering behaviours and trying things.
- Could be more creative.
- Gets frustrated easily in training sessions.

I also use it as a general tool to fine-tune arousal levels in balance with the 'reward nothing' game. This game is lots of fun; it hones your training skills and encourages your dog to think for himself.

Here's how to play:

- Prepare 10 treats.
- Sit down in front of your dog.
- Every time your dog moves or offers a behaviour/trick – reward him!
- Now wait until he offers a different movement/behaviour/trick and reward again.

The rules are:

1. You reward your dog for movement! This should be any behaviour he offers, no matter how tiny! This is where training yourself comes into it. You need to develop the skills so that you notice and reward the tiniest head, paw and body movement, as well as the more overt behaviours that your dog may already know and offer.

2. You must not reward your dog for the same movement twice in a row. This encourages him to keep offering different behaviours, creating value for movement, upping arousal, building resilience to frustration, and developing and nurturing the creativity with which he approaches situations This is the means of developing a hugely flexible learner.

The 'reward anything' game is brilliant for building arousal, motivation, creativity, and the determination to keep trying new and different things in training. It tips the arousal balance towards higher arousal and is a great warm-up exercise before a training session or a competition run.

I developed these games to work with arousal in all kinds of cases – and I would be lost without them! They are so simple, yet the effects are profound. They are the opposite of one another in terms of the game itself, and the effects that they have on the dogs. Play these games at home, take them on the road and start applying them in different situations. Work on your training skills, and your ability to read your dog – and the successes will follow. Happy dog training!

3. BEHAVIOURS AND AROUSAL

The training you have already undertaken can become part of your arousal manipulation toolkit. How can that work? Well, think about trick training...

Tricks are the often-neglected performance-enhancing freebie that everybody needs to use more. This is because each trick you teach inherently increases or decreases arousal. This depends on a number of factors, including the amount of movement or stillness involved, as already discussed. You can make use of this in training by teaching tricks that decrease arousal, termed 'off-switch behaviours', and tricks that increase arousal, termed 'on-switch behaviours'.

OFF-SWITCH BEHAVIOURS

These include any behaviour that serves to reduce your dog's arousal level. The key is observation, as you need to determine what behaviours are off-switches for your dog. Observe the effect on his behaviour, his head space, and his subsequent choices when he performs the behaviour. Off-

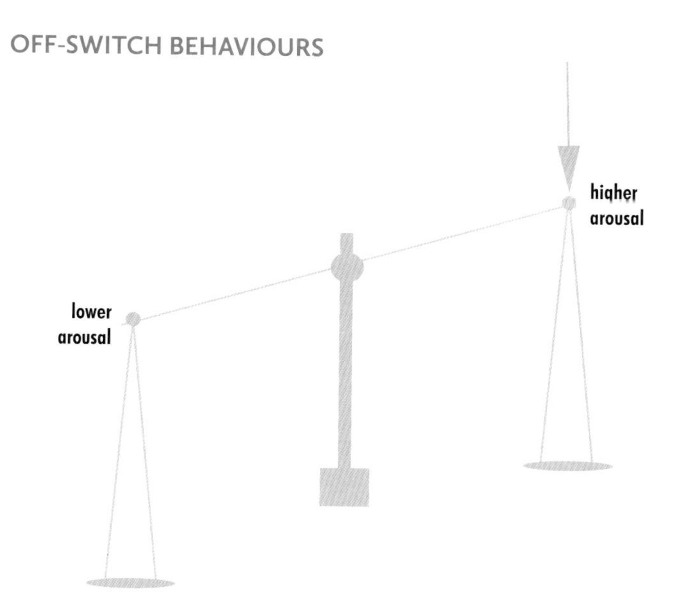

Teaching off-switch behaviours – which may include paw-targeting or boundary games – will decrease arousal levels.

switch behaviours are typically those that are taught with:

- Calmness.
- Precision.

...and may involve a degree of stillness!

This means that you can train and develop new off-switch behaviours in addition to those your dog knows already.

Depending on your dog's individual response, off-switch behaviours may include:

- Chin targeting.
- Shoulder targeting.
- Paw targeting.
- Middle.
- Boundary games.
- Precise retrieve to hand.
- Sit, down, stand chains.

To train an off-switch behaviour, your dog need to be in the right mindset, which may require starting the session with the 'reward nothing' game.

Middle

For me, training the 'middle' behaviour does far more than act as an off-switch – although that is a good enough reason in its own right. This behaviour allows you to:

- Get your dog into safety quickly.
- Provide a safe haven for a worried dog, close to your legs.
- Allows you to position your dog (for example at the start of an agility run or for veterinary/physio examinations).
- Build impulse control when used as a middle extension game (see page 154).

Middle involves teaching your dog to move to a sit position

between your legs. The behaviour requires precision, but it is also a great way to get your dog out of a situation where he might be feeling anxious or threatened. It is an absolute necessity for busy environments.

This is how I train it:

- To shape this behaviour, start by rewarding your dog for turning around your leg and going behind you. You can do this by rewarding any movement your dog makes in that direction and delivering the reward at the back of your legs and, eventually, between your legs.
- Work on this this until your dog is consistently heading around your leg and then between your legs. At this point, the reward should always be placed in the final position – between your legs.
- Build duration for maintaining the position between your legs by providing a rapid rate of reinforcement in this position. Then work on reducing the rate of reinforcement while your dog stays in place.

Now you can work on the end behaviour – a sit! You can do this in the following ways:

- Shape the sit by marking and rewarding weight shifts backwards until your dog sits.
- Cue a sit. Repeat the chain a few times, cueing the sit and then waiting for your dog to offer it.
- Cue a nose target with your hand above your dog's head so that he sits when targeting.
- Build duration into maintaining the sit position between your legs by manipulating the rate of reinforcement again.

Remember that you do not want to build frustration or arousal when you are building this behaviour. The key is to keep the rate of reinforcement at a reasonable level.

Middle Extension Games

Middle-Control

My dog, Betcha, loves this game!

- Start by engaging your dog in play with a toy.
- Then hold the toy in front of you and ask for "middle". Your dog must get into position, and wait for the release before he can grab the toy.
- If he breaks position, flip the toy out of the way.

This is a great real-life proofing game, as in everyday situations he will be faced with all kinds of distractions that lie ahead of him and must wait for release from the position.

Middle-Whip

- Engage your dog in chasing the whip-it (see page 59).
- Make the whip go still (which should curtail your dog's movement, and impulse control should be offered as in the whip it game) and ask for "middle".
- If he goes into position, you can activate the toy again, and then release him straight forward to chase it again. If he fails to call off the toy, flip the whip-it out of the way.

Middle-Behaviours

- Ask your dog for "middle" and then ask for behaviour chains (sit, down, stand, bed, sit pretty, etc.) while you are facing straight ahead.

This builds great reliability in arousal, independence from your body position and flexibility as your dog is changing what he usually does in that position.

Body Targeting

This is a great off-switch behaviour to train, and you can use the formula to teach any body part targeting. Body targeting involves your dog targeting a specific body part to your hand, e.g. his nose, chin, shoulder – you name it! It involves three steps:

1. Value priming
2. Place away and capture
3. Add the cue

1. Value priming

This is to ensure that your dog is not only comfortable with hand placement on the body part (let's use chin targeting as the example), but also sees it as a predictor of something fun or tasty! You want to build value for this, so that your dog is keen to use his chin to seek out your hand.

- Start by placing your hand under your dog's chin, marking the moment, and rewarding. Use super tasty food or an extra special toy and work slowly as this may feel strange to some dogs.
- At this point, add duration into the targeting with a rapid-fire rate of reinforcement. You can reward directly to the mouth, maintaining chin contact with your hand.
- Work on this until your dog shows super desire for resting his chin in your hand. In time, when you withhold the treat for a couple of seconds, your dog will begin to press more firmly into your hand. This shows you are ready to move on to the next step.

2. Place away and capture

- Place your hand slightly away from your dog's chin and capture the moment when he seeks out your hand with his chin.
- Work on this until your dog understands the desired behaviour, i.e. the moment he targets his chin to your hand. The key is to build lots of value for your hand so that he is actively seeking it out. Do not progress until he shows you that he understands the behaviour.

- Now build distance by moving your hand further away. Progress in small stages, gradually increasing the distance, and then later adding side-to-side motion.

3. Add the cue

- When you have established the final behaviour – and you can guarantee that your dog will offer the behaviour when you present your hand – add a cue! This ensures that when you say your chosen cue, "chin" for example, your dog will target your hand with his chin. Give your verbal cue, present your hand, reward for the correct behaviour – simple!

> ***TOP TIP!***
> *Adding a release cue to this behaviour can be lots of fun! You can use your normal release cue (or invent another one), and then disconnect hand from your dog. He will begin to predict the release cue as the end of the behaviour, and will disengage himself, once you have given the cue. Reward the release every time!*

ON-SWITCH BEHAVIOURS

This embraces any behaviour that triggers arousal after it has been cued.

Generally, on-switch behaviours are those that:

- You have trained using a fast-paced and light-mannered approach.
- Your dog naturally enjoys.
- Are associated with huge reinforcement opportunities.
- Involve movement or positions your dog enjoys.

In this instance, you are aiming for the opposite effect of off-switch behaviours. Both on-switch and off-switch behaviours are equally valuable, but it is the combination that is truly powerful in terms of manipulating arousal levels, and thereby enhancing learning and performance.

Depending on your own, individual dog, examples of on-switch behaviours may include:

- Left and right spins.
- Jumping
- Barking (I train barking using the "show me you want it" game, see page 99)
- Nose targets.
- Leg weaving.
- Circling and wrapping poles.

Circle

I like to shape this trick so it's important to decide the direction of the circle before you start.

- Before beginning to shape the behaviour, I get the dog used to chasing a toy or food around my body.
- To shape "circle", mark and reward turns, and steps towards behind you, to start with. Place the treat or toy behind you, moving it by degrees as your dog learns the behaviour.

TOP TIP!

Consider how you apply your reinforcement! If you are wanting speed and excitement in the final behaviour, then roll the reward (food or toy) in the direction that you are rewarding your dog for heading!

- Continue with this until your dog is consistently heading around your body, resulting in a full circle!
- To add more speed and excitement, restrain your dog (as long as he is ok with this!) and release him to perform it. Make sure you have the reinforcer waiting for him to build great value into the behaviour.
- When you are happy with the final behaviour, introduce your cue ("circle", "roundabout", "rotate") just before your dog performs the full behaviour and reward handsomely. If you have built a restrain into the beginning of the behaviour, give the verbal cue just before releasing him. Reinforce and work towards cueing without the restrain.

Bear in mind, what may be an on-switch for one dog may be an off-switch for another dog, and vice versa, so watch your dog for signs of arousal post-behaviour.

Training on- and off-switch behaviours from scratch will give you more control over the outcome as you are developing the mindset you want the behaviour to produce, prior to training it. However, every trick your dog already knows will represent either an on-switch or an off-switch to some extent – so go and play around with them in your training!

CHAPTER 14
AROUSAL UP, AROUSAL DOWN

The analogy of a light switch in describing high arousal versus low arousal works well when it comes to describing dog behavior and training. When a light switch is brand new, it can be a little stiff to switch one way or both ways. This might mean it's easy to switch the light on, but it requires more effort to switch it off, or vice versa. As the switch is used more often, the process becomes easier – effectively, through practice.

Exactly the same applies to switching between high and low arousal in dogs. The more a dog practises moving at speed from low arousal to high arousal, and high arousal to low arousal, the easier the switch will be to operate in the future – the switch gets looser. In dog training terms, this is really exciting as it means we can develop a dog's ability to switch between high and low arousal quickly, which is vital for performance dogs.

GAMES TO PLAY

There are a number of games you can play with your dog that will help you to loosen the switch:

Arousal Up, Arousal Down (and Down and Up...)

This game does what it says on the tin; it is something I start to play very early on with a young puppy, and I will then top it up throughout the dog's life.

- Start by getting your dog really excited about something – that might be chasing you, wrapping a tree, playing tug, doing some physical wrestling – whatever gets your dog really high.

- Disengage and wait for your dog to lower his arousal and calm down. You can stroke him gently and reward him for increasing calmness, and also to promote further calmness.
- Then, you guessed it, restart the game! Reward your dog for using his off-switch with switching it back on again.

High Up to Reward Nothing

This game is the same as above but, when ending the high arousal game, you immediately switch to the 'reward nothing' game. Initially this is challenging, so you will need to give clear signals to indicate the end of the exciting event. I find that if I go from standing to sitting cross-legged, and use subtle signals such dropping shoulders or slow blinking, the dog finds it easy to pick up the correct message.

Arousal Down to Reward Anything

This is the opposite of the game described above, as you start with a calm, settled dog and transition to the 'reward anything' game. The key is to not be too picky with the behaviours you reward. Simply mark any behaviour where movement is involved – a tiny paw lift will do to begin with!

Boundary to Work to Boundary

This is my favourite of all these games!

- Start by playing some boundary games; call your dog from the boundary (bed/crate/from across the room) and do some high arousal work, for example, barrel wrapping or race to a dead toy in this.
- Now end the session and go and sit by the boundary. When your dog returns to the boundary, stroke him and calmly deliver some food, rewarding him for the arousal *down* element of the game.

This not only develops the concept and skill of switching to lower arousal, it is a real-life applicable exercise. Life is effectively all about transitioning from boundary to boundary – with some fun along the way!

AROUSAL AND EMOTION

Arousal and emotion are hugely intertwined; emotion is, in part, a product of arousal levels, as I will discuss shortly. But first I want to focus on how arousal does not only influence emotion but how arousal, itself, can mask negative emotions (such as fear and frustration), allowing them to go unnoticed for long periods by which time things can spiral out of control.

OVER-AROUSAL, FEAR, FRUSTRATION – WHO KNOWS?

In order to understand our failure to identify arousal, let's revisit how over-arousal can look (see page 162).

This list highlights a huge downside of over-arousal – the biggest in my opinion. Why? Well, ask yourself the following questions:

How does **frustration** look?

How does **fear** look?

Now, how does **over-arousal** look?

The problem is that each of the three emotions can look exactly the same. In fact, the way a dog chooses to cope with frustration, fear or over-arousal is often identical. It is less common for him to select different coping strategies for different underlying negative emotional states. Therefore, dogs that regularly become over-aroused cannot be distinguished from those that are exhibiting fear responses, feeling anxious or frustrated.

examples of the clues of over-arousal		
barking	howling	growling
hiding	escaping	pulling on lead
lagging on lead	chasing	trembling/shaking
being restless	pacing	being vigilant
circling	seeking out people	increasing owner attachment
salivating	lip licking	panting
a stronger/harder mouth when taking treats	cheek puffing	yawning
staring	ground sniffing	self grooming
scratching	any form of aggression	lead lunging
biting lead	playing, aggressing or staring at invisible things	unresponsiveness
freezing	important disinterest in treats that are normally enjoyed	important inability to respond to learnt cues

This is very important as it means that the development of behavioural problems can go unnoticed for long periods; even worse, they may never be identified or the motivation for undesirable behaviour is completely misunderstood.

HOW TO BUILD AN EMOTION

Understanding animal (and human) emotions is a growing field in science, but it is rarely applied to dogs, dog training and dog sports. I like to explain emotion and arousal through an adaptation of the dimensional model, devised by human psychologist, James Russell, in 2003. His dimensional model considers emotion to be determined by a combination of two things:

- Arousal level: low or high.
- Valence: positive (attraction to an event) or negative (aversion to an event).

COMPONENTS OF EMOTION

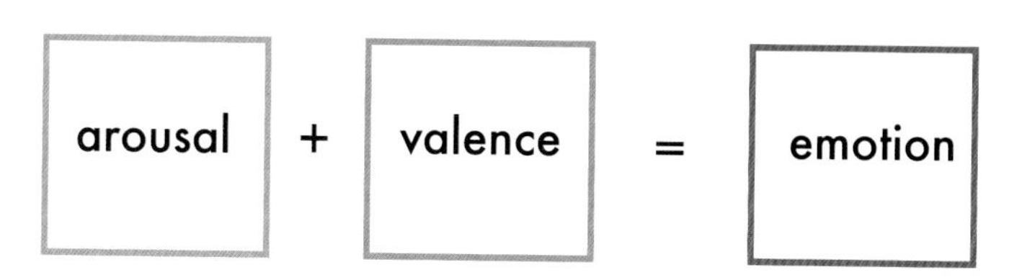

An emotion is triggered by valence – a positive or negative response to an event – and its associated arousal level.

BASIC FORMULA

Valence is a term to describe the nature of the emotion (good or bad) and is the result of whether the trigger or stimulus is appetitive (desirable) or aversive (undesirable). Emotions are made up of a valence (positive or negative) and an associated arousal level. Positive valence emotions would include: excitement, happiness and calmness, in order of decreasing arousal. Negative valence emotions would be: fear, anxiety, worry and uneasiness, again in order of decreasing arousal.

DIMENSIONAL MODEL

This model allows you to predict the emotion that will result from a specific situation. Check out the following scenario: your dog is in a state of excitement/high arousal because he is out on a walk, or has maybe just had a game of tug. Then a barking, lunging dog appears, providing an undesirable stimulus/trigger, i.e. negative valence. The combination of

DIMENSIONAL MODEL

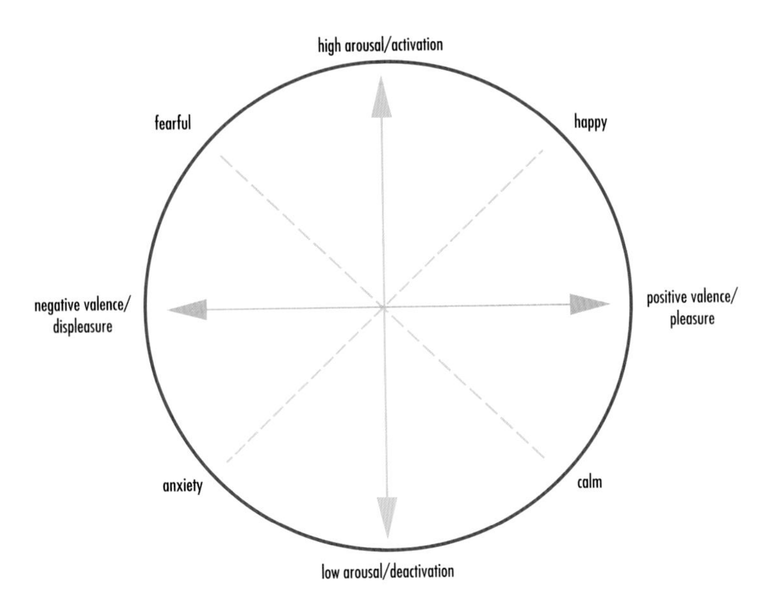

If you consider a situation in terms of negative or positive valence, and the level of arousal your dog is experiencing, you will be able to predict his likely behaviour.

emotions your dog is experiencing results in a response of fear rather than sadness, worry or low level anxiety.

FEAR FORMULA

Now you can begin to imagine the effect of specific environments and situations on companion and on performance dogs, which will be made worse if they are over-aroused. Take an agility show for example. This is an environment that has hundreds of desirable and undesirable triggers that could easily result in skyrocketing arousal, which might be evidenced as extreme excitement or extreme fear responses. This might be evidenced in behaviour such as barking, lunging, or grabbing a tug toy continuously. Have you seen dogs behave like this in competition?

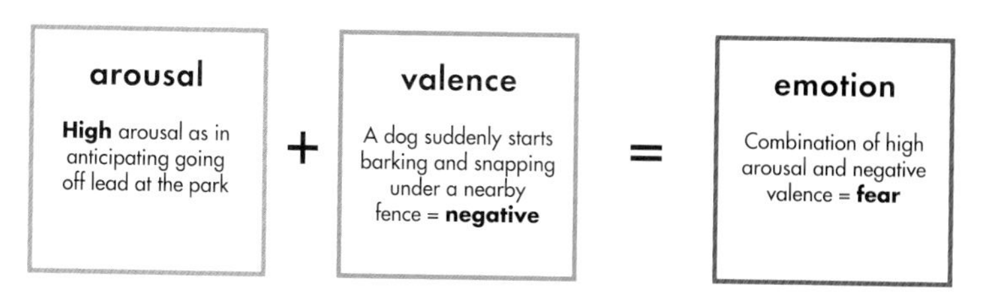

arousal
High arousal as in anticipating going off lead at the park
+
valence
A dog suddenly starts barking and snapping under a nearby fence = **negative**
=
emotion
Combination of high arousal and negative valence = **fear**

This is what happens when high arousal and negative valence collide...

THE FOUR BOXES

	negative valence	positive valence
high arousal	fear	excitement
low arousal	anxiety	calmness

In terms of emotion, dogs can be in any one of these four boxes.

The dimensional model (see page 163) is incredibly useful in dog training and behaviour as it allows us to not only to predict the emotional status of dogs, but also allows us to target the approach to training and behaviour modification based on the individual components of the emotion.

For example, if your dog had just reacted to another dog, a person or a sound, and was in a fearful state, how would you attempt to modify his behaviour to help him return to a state of balance? You would need to do two things in the aftermath of the event: firstly reduce arousal, and secondly add positive outcomes in the situation.

FROM FEAR TO CALMNESS

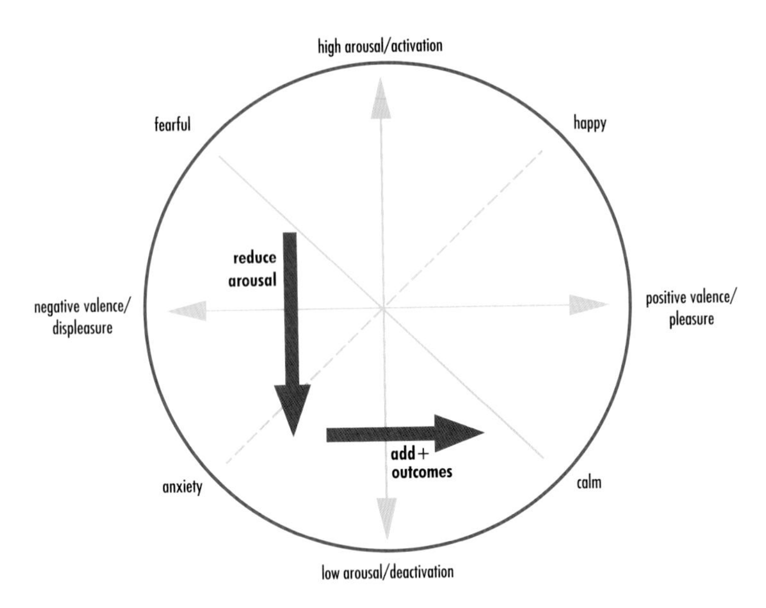

You can modify behaviour by lowering arousal and introducing positive outcomes.

This might take the form of taking the dog away from the situation and playing the 'reward nothing' game to both reduce arousal and switch the valence of the emotional state to a positive one by providing positive ('appetitive') outcomes – in this case food!

Equally, you may want to modify your dog's behaviour prior to an agility run so that he feels positive and excited (see The Four Boxes, top right box – page 165). If you identify him as being calm (bottom right box), then you would simply up the arousal, which may be asking for some on-switch behaviours, such as spinning or barking. However, if you identified him as being worried or anxious (bottom left box), it could be very dangerous to add arousal (see From Unease to Fear, page 167).

FROM UNEASE TO FEAR

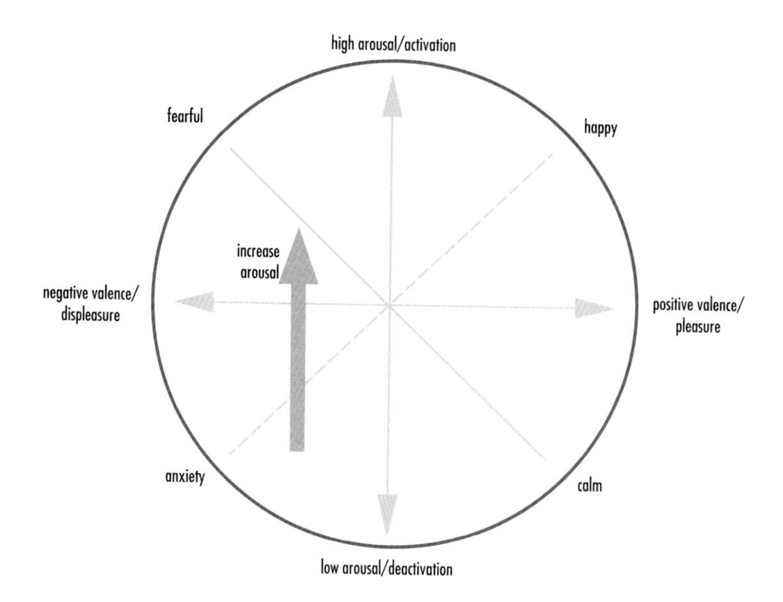

Allowing arousal levels to increase when a dog is feeling anxious can have a disastrous effect.

The first step is to bring him across to the 'happy land' before upping the arousal. It is crucial that this is done in the correct order to avoid engaging fear, and all the behaviours and problems that come with it.

DEALING WITH FRUSTRATION

This is a powerful emotion that can take on a number of guises; it can go unnoticed for long periods and is frequently misunderstood.

Frustration is the emotion that ensues when something is anticipated but does not happen. It would be the emotion you would experience if your pay cheque was late, or if your spouse promised to put the rubbish out for collection and then failed to do it.

With reference to dogs, frustration would be experienced if the outcome they were expecting is delayed, or if it doesn't happen at all. This might happen in relation to:

- Being rewarded in a training session.
- Mealtimes.
- Going for a walk.
- Greeting the dog/person/rabbit on the other side of the street.
- Taking the tunnel rather than the A frame in agility, or the timing of handling cues.

Further reading for the science fans...

Russell, J. A. 2003, Core affect and the psychological construction of emotion, *Psychological Review*, 110, 145.

Figures are adaptations from Russell (2003) from Tom Mitchell's clinical and theoretical work.

CHAPTER 15
TOLERANCE OF FRUSTRATION

Frustration can manifest in a variety of ways and, worryingly, the behaviours I see in a frustrated dog overlap completely with those of a scared, worried, anxious or over-aroused/excited dog. Each cause can mask the others – whether that be fear being misinterpreted as frustration or frustration for over-arousal – it leads to problems going unnoticed or the wrong decisions being made. This is one of the reasons why building an appropriate tolerance to things not happening when expected is so crucial.

There are other reasons to build a tolerance to frustration, because:

- It enhances learning and performance by creating a dog that is more able to cope with failure – and can even overcome it.
- It builds a better tolerance for when we mess up or are too slow in our rewarding or our cueing, whether that is in training or competition, and creates a learner that is generally more resilient to handler mistakes.
- It creates a dog that is more resilient to changes in routine and deviations from expectation in day-to-day life.

At the extreme end of poor tolerance of frustration, I have seen dogs become completely unnerved by changes in routine.

This could be a change in the daily programme – not being walked because the dog's owner is injured, or something as simple as the water bowl being empty when it should be full – both can lead to extreme behavioural responses.

Typically, a dog that has a poor tolerance of frustration:

- Gives up in a training session.
- Is reluctant to try new choices.
- Fails to think through a struggle, for example inability to cope with lack of reward in a shaping session where things are not going well.
- Tries to cope with the frustration by doing anything from sniffing to zoomies – and may even resort to biting.

FRUSTRATION AND REACTIVITY

Frustration is not a pleasant emotion. If your dog frequently experiences frustration in a given situation – for example, he is continually prevented interacting with another dog or person – this commonly transforms from the negative emotion of frustration to the negative emotion of fear.

A common cause of dog-dog reactivity is inappropriate play behaviour and an inability to effectively interact with other dogs in a mutually rewarding way. Why does it happen? Frustration! I am sure you have all seen a dog barking and circling another dog because he cannot get his 'mate' to play. As described above, this frustration can transform into fear as time goes on. In addition the frustration behaviours – circling and barking at the other dog – are often unnerving and may cause the other dog to react, resulting in a secondary negative association.

We, as owners are not wholly responsible for the frustration in our dogs' lives. It may be another animal (e.g. the cat that won't run away to enable a game of chase), or even an object (e.g. the treat dispenser that isn't quite as easy as anticipated).

Therefore, developing a tolerance of frustration not only benefits interactions between us and our dogs, but also interactions between our dogs and the outside world, reducing the possibility of reactivity and making us one step closer to developing calm and happy dogs.

DO WE NEED FRUSTRATION IN TRAINING?

This is a really interesting question. Frustration feels uncomfortable and is never welcomed – but it is the emotion that drives us to our greatest achievements. If the outcome you want isn't happening, you try harder or you try something different to reach your goal.

To validate the use of frustration in training, you need to weigh up the pros and cons:

AGAINST

In a training session, removing frustration – or, at least, minimising it – is beneficial. Any time you cue a behaviour in which frustration was repeatedly involved in the learning process, you inevitably trigger that same emotion. Triggering a high arousal, negative emotion is not ideal when you are working in a complex competition environment, so minimising frustration in training sessions is often desirable.

FOR

But you also need to bear in mind that life is frustrating, and training can be a frustrating business for both dog and handler. Anticipated outcomes and events may not happen at the right time, or they might not happen at all. In addition, some dogs come into this world with an extremely low tolerance of frustration. Such a dog is frustrated, and even distressed, when anticipated events fail to occur and, by their nature, these are often dogs that anticipate a lot. But life is not predictable, so it is only fair to prepare a dog so he can cope with this.

In the sports arena, the chain of events, behaviours and cues is designed to differ every time, so a tolerance to change/frustration should be considered a prerequisite.

In summary, a tolerance of frustration is absolutely vital. It makes the difference between a dog that learns and performs to the best of his ability, and a dog that struggles; it marks a dog that is a pleasure to live with, and the dog that is uneasy – sometimes to the extent of developing behavioural problems.

Dogs that lack a tolerance to frustration are described as "impatient", or they are given the classic labels of being "bossy" or "stubborn". This is because when such a dog is faced with a frustrating situation – not getting an anticipated reward, for example – he will opt to shut down, leave the situation or become reactive rather than upping his game and working through the challenge.

I have devised a series of games that build tolerance and encourage a dog's ability to work effectively when faced with frustration. They involve setting up situations where something desirable is not immediately accessible – but eventually materialises when the right choices are made. The key is to progress step-by-step, building the frustration a little at a time. You do not want to put your dog in a situation where he practises zero tolerance. For this reason, I have outlined the games (below) in order of increasing difficulty:

Treat Dispensers

Treat dispensers, such as kongs, food puzzles, and even some long-lasting treats/chews are great for building a tolerance of frustration – and do not necessarily require direct involvement from you.

When a client tells me their dog ignores food puzzles/kongs, the assumption is that the dog is "bored", "lazy" or "stubborn". In fact, the reason is often because of a low tolerance of frustration, i.e. the dog stops engaging when he is not immediately presented with what he is expecting. The key to progressing this game is to manipulate the degree of difficulty in terms of achieving the end goal – getting the food.

This is how I introduce a kong to a dog that has very low tolerance of frustration. It needs to be done over many sessions:

- Kong on floor, kibble at the side.
- Kong on floor, kibble in the mouth of the kong.
- One piece of kibble inside kong.
- A quantity of kibble inside kong.
- Food paste in mouth of kong.
- Food paste plus kibble in kong.
- Wet dog food (I would use something very smelly, such as green tripe) in mouth of kong.
- Kong packed with wet dog food.
- Paste in the mouth of the kong and filled with frozen food.
- Kong filled with frozen food.

I work through all of these steps sequentially – no matter the level of tolerance of frustration. In cases where building tolerance to frustration is a priority, I would incorporate the food dispenser as part of a reinforcement-rich lifestyle so a proportion of the daily food ration is delivered by this method.

Find It!

This is such a simple game and really useful for building tolerance to frustration. There are countless variations – your imagination is the only limiting factor!

To play this game, your dog needs to be separated from a reward (food or toy), and then he has to work to find it. It is especially effective when your dog can see the item. A variation I play very early on (even before pups go to their new homes) is to place a food bowl on the other side of an open puppy pen.

Puppies with a low tolerance of frustration will throw themselves at the bars, vocalise or completely give in. These pups need to spend time on easier food-finding games before tackling this one. Others will pause for a moment, assess the situation and then begin to try different things until they figure out how to reach their desired item. Other variations of the game include:

- Concealing food or a toy under an upturned bowl.
- Hiding food or a toy somewhere in a room.
- Asking a friend to restrain your dog and hide food or a toy in the environment.

...and so on – the opportunities are endless!

Scatter Feeding

This a great game to make your dog's dinner work to your advantage when you don't have the time or energy to engage in an active training session. In all my training and behaviour work, my aim is to use every possible opportunity to benefit learning – and this game fits the bill to perfection!

Instead of giving your dog his rations in a food bowl (which he anticipates) simply scatter it in the garden. Sniffing out the food builds a tolerance to frustration as the reward is self-evident – but it does not occur immediately. Searching for food in this way also serves as a great way to empty the arousal bucket, reducing arousal in an active and productive way, and a fun activity which is enjoyed by all dogs.

With both of the above games, the aim is for the dog to persevere with the activity and work with it from start to finish, without any indicators of frustration such as barking or leaving, but also to show joy in doing it. Inevitably, there will be some degree of frustration experienced at times, but, if the dog is then able to bring himself back into a thinking headspace and continue, I don't intervene. If, however, the dog is becoming increasingly frustrated, I would look to distract him from the activity to interrupt his behaviour, and then think about how I could change things next time.

NOTE FOR BREEDERS

Interacting with treat dispensers, playing find it, and engaging in scatter feeding are all games that can and should be done with puppies before they go to their new homes. I introduce these games from around four weeks of age and build up the difficulty level until the pups are ready to leave.

Prior to the four weeks of age point, I set up a series of simple tasks, again making them progressively more difficult. For example, when the pups are just a few days old, I remove them from their mother's teats and place them a short distance away so they have to find their way back, and are rewarded with their mother's milk.

I extend this game by placing small obstacles – such as a blanket or a pillow, which are easy to negotiate – between the pups and their mum. I would then experiment with introducing an object that has a different texture, such as a deflated dimpled wobble cushion.

I have found that these games are hugely beneficial in developing a good tolerance to frustration before puppies go to their new homes, helping them to become adaptable and well-balanced individuals.

Push Back and Run Away

This game, and the game called restrained recalls (see below) can be played with puppies from around six weeks of age. I also use them with dogs that are new to concept training.

Play this game by:

- Getting some food in your right hand, and then positioning your dog on your right side. Restrain him by holding your right hand (with the food), cupped against his chest.
- Using your right hand, gently push him back and set off at run.
- When your dog catches up, feed him the food.

You can build the intensity of this game up by gently pushing your dog further back. This engages the opposition reflex, propelling him forwards, building focus, and tolerance of frustration all at the same time!

Restrained Recalls

For this game, you need to enlist the help of a friend who will restrain your dog while you walk away and then give the recall cue. To start with, leave your dog a short distance and allow him to be released immediately. Gradually extend the distance you leave him and increase the time before he is released. This not only encourages a good recall, but also builds tolerance to frustration.

If you are training by yourself, play this game with a long line attached to your dog's harness and restrain him by looping the line around a tree so you have a head-start before releasing him.

When I first played this game with Illy, my Standard Poodle, I discovered that she had extremely low tolerance of frustration and struggled with any restraint, or barrier, that kept her from whatever it was she wanted. Initially, the issue centred on the fact that Illy only wanted me! Progressing the game in simple steps was a real lifesaver, and made a massive difference to her threshold for tolerating frustration – and to our on-going relationship.

Restrained recalls are one of the first "go to" games at puppy classes, but for many dogs with a low tolerance of frustration, this game is far too much to start with. Subjecting a youngster to this level of frustration is likely to lead to a bad outcome, ranging from reduced learning and performance to shutdown, disengagement or, at worse, an episode of reactivity.

If the dog shows any level of disliking the restraint or distance by trying to escape, going beyond just pushing forward in anticipation, I would look to bring the difficulty level down and build back up by considering any, or all, of the following changes:

- Brief touch of the dog's harness and immediately let go.
- Brief hold of the dog's harness and then immediately let go.
- Attach a long line to the harness and, as the dog pushes on, feed it through my hands to provide a small amount of resistance – but allowing continuous progress.
- Reduce the distance I lead out on.

Race to Toy/Dinner

This game involves setting up a toy, a food pile or a bowl of food ahead of your dog, restraining him for a varying amount of time, and then releasing him to race to the resource!

For advanced development of tolerance of frustration, ask your dog for a behaviour (e.g. down) or even a behaviour chain (e.g. sit, down, left spin, bow) before releasing him to the toy/food.

In this game, I would aim for the dog to practise none of the behaviours that may be indicators of frustration. If for example, he loses energy or begins sniffing, I would pause, bring the energy back up and check that the dog is able to bring himself back into a thinking headspace and carry on. In order to build a tolerance of frustration, the dog must – to a certain extent

– experience the emotion of frustration (due to lack of immediate, expected outcomes), but this should not be excessive so as to cause the opposite of what we want to achieve.

Pole Wrapping

Pole wrapping (see page 94) is a great way of building tolerance to frustration, as it is easy to ask for repetitions, and to be unpredictable when you reward.

A dog can often tolerate and work through frustration if:

- The 'work' involves continuation of something he is already doing, i.e. continuing to wrap the pole.
- The 'work" involves movement rather than stillness/ precision.

GRIT AND TOLERANCE OF FRUSTRATION

You may be finding that the difference between grit and tolerance of frustration is quite difficult to grasp – and I agree! The two are inextricably linked, so separating one from another in concept training is almost impossible, which is illustrated in the overlap of games that build each concept.

I believe that frustration is inevitable in life and training to a certain degree. As concept trainers, we therefore need to do two things in order to reach optimum learning and performance:

- Create a tolerance of not getting an outcome (for example, food) that is expected, and for not getting the outcome right in the first instance.
- When frustration is encountered – the reward is longer term than anticipated, for example – we encourage the dog to push through the frustration, try harder, try something different and certainly never shut down. Grit building creates a dog that opts to cope with frustration, works harder to find answers – and is 100 per cent cool about it!

CAUSE AND EFFECT

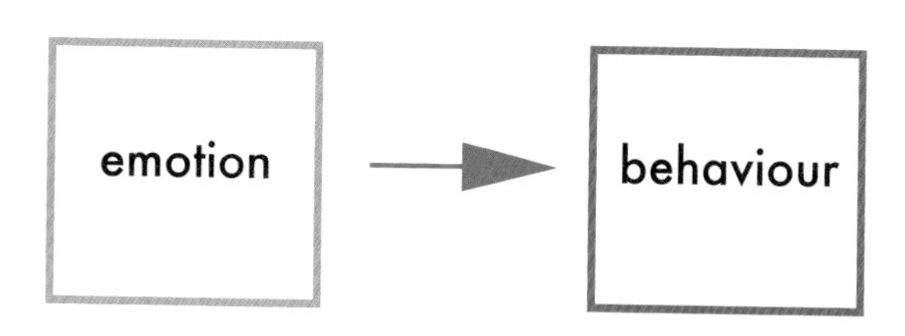

The emotion a dog is experiencing will have a direct impact on the way he behaves.

EMOTION TO BEHAVIOURS

Emotions cause, influence and change behaviours. The typical behaviours of a calm dog are very different from those seen in an excited, over-aroused dog. It helps to look at the interaction between emotion and behaviour in the following way:

- Whenever a dog feels an emotion, he walks over to the behaviour shelving system in his brain, and picks up the box labelled with that emotion. He opens it up and picks a behaviour.
- The behaviours that come out of the fear behaviour box may be lunging, barking, growling, freezing or goofing around, whereas the behaviours that come out of the calmness behaviour box may be lying down, sitting, sleeping or slowly looking around

As already discussed, the behaviours that come out of the fear, frustration and over-arousal behaviour boxes are often very similar.

Initially, the behaviour a dog chooses might be random but, as he gets older, experiences more emotions and responds accordingly, he will select behaviours that he has found most effective when he has been in the same or similar situations. For example, he will pick a behaviour that most effectively reduces his negative feelings of fear/anxiety, whether that

FINDING A BALANCE

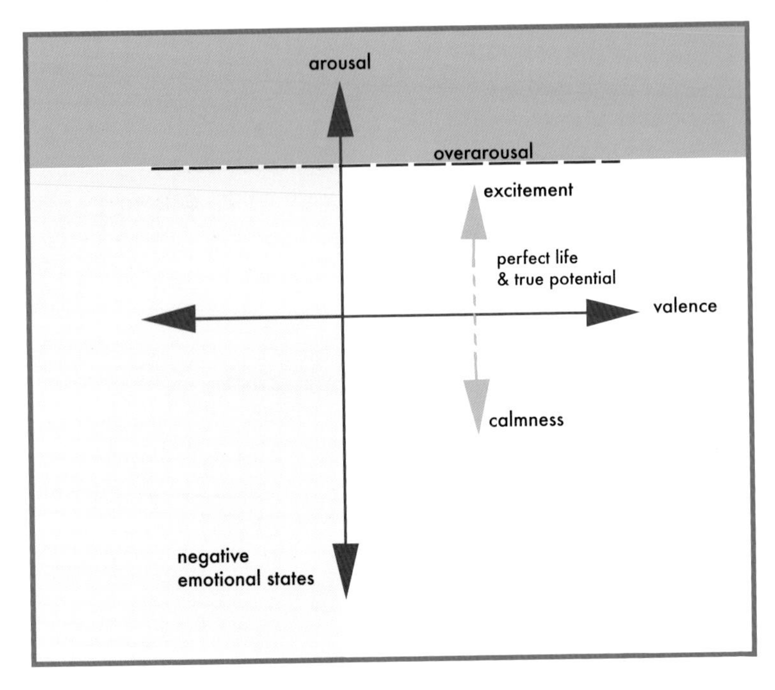

If a dog is in balance – not over-aroused or affected by negative associations – he has the ability to achieve his true potential.

is barking, lunging or fly snapping. These are his 'coping strategies', something that we can relate to very closely. In human terms, coping strategies might be going for a walk, exercising at the gym, or training your dog. Alternatively, they may take the form of opening a bottle of wine, eating cake or smoking. Some strategies are less appropriate than others – and so it is with dogs...

ABNORMAL REPETITIVE BEHAVIOURS

Behaviour problems that are expressed in abnormal repetitive behaviours (ARBs), such as tail chasing, self-mutilation, and light chasing, are still examples of coping strategies, despite their undesirable outcomes.

They are seemingly performed with a high degree of motivation and intent and are therefore often labelled 'obsessive' or 'compulsive'. However, it is much more appropriate (and practical) to look at these seemingly inappropriate and extreme behaviours as being something that has been simply selected from a behaviour box, just as any other coping strategy may develop. This may have been at random and proved to be effective, or the dog may have a genetic predisposition to selecting a certain behaviour, for example light-stalking Border Collies or flank-sucking Dobermanns.

The only difference with these abnormal repetitive behaviours, compared to other behavioural coping strategies, is that the dog has chosen a behaviour that we find unusual and perhaps distressing. Once established as coping strategies for whatever emotion has triggered the response, these ARBs quickly become the behaviour of choice when a dog is presented with fear, frustration, over-arousal or excitement – regardless of where the behaviour originated from.

The key to working with ARBs starts with identifying the emotion that initially triggered the behaviour, and the many emotions that now trigger it.

REACTIVITY

Reactivity is the term given to dogs that pick out behaviours from the fear, frustration or over-arousal boxes and use them as coping strategies that are inappropriate in day-to-day life – lunging, vocalising, biting, for example. It is important to bear in mind that the intensity, or type of behaviour, does not necessarily bear any correlation with the intensity of the emotion experienced by the dog.

My clinical experience backs up research that shows that dogs with more active behaviours, such as lunging or barking, cope better with their negative emotional status than those that adopt a more passive approach – freezing, for example.

In summary, you can reach your dog's potential in learning, performance and happiness by doing two things:

- **Firstly**, avoiding over-arousal. This means:
  - Manipulate arousal effectively to avoid over-arousal (see Chapter 13).
  - Creating a low basal arousal level (Calmness, see Chapter 10).
  - Developing resilience to high arousal and an ability to think at all arousal levels (Thinking in arousal, see Chapter 12).
  - Creating a dog that can switch between arousal levels effectively to allow quicker lowering of arousal after exciting or scary events (Arousal up, arousal down, see Chapter 14).
- **Secondly**, communicating to your dog that everything in the world is good – regardless of whether it is new, old and strange – to ensure he stays in the 'happy land' of positive valence.

CHAPTER 16
TRAINING FOR OPTIMISM

In the context of dogs and dog training, the definition of optimism is that when a dog is presented with something new or slightly strange, he presumes it to be something *good* rather than something to be worried about!

This learning is huge. For me, optimism makes the difference between an effortless canine companion to share the world with, and one that is the complete opposite. Optimism is a fundamental concept that dogs today must have in order to be successful. An optimistic dog is not reactive; he is confident and he is a keen learner. A huge benefit, especially in relation to optimistic sports dogs, is that they are a pleasure to train. When faced with complex and potentially scary environments, the optimistic sports dog has no hang-ups – he simply believes everything will be super!

Considering that most behaviour problems (and many sport dog problems) relate to underlying negative emotional responses to things in the environment, it goes without saying that optimism is 100 per cent necessary for success. Optimistic dogs are confident, learn readily and are not overcome by struggles, whether that be a tricky training challenge or a potentially worrying event.

Optimism and pessimism are intrinsic characteristics in animals. In a survival context, animals that are more pessimistic live longer, reproduce more, and protect their young more effectively, leading to perpetuation of this characteristic. Why is this? It is because these individuals guard against danger. They are always on red alert, and it pays off because there will be a time when the rustling bush hides a predator, proving that running away is the best strategy to adopt! In the same situation, the optimist may not make the right choice – and his naivety will cost him dear.

However, in a domesticated setting, pessimism has a detrimental effect on both companion and performance dogs because it creates a mentality of presuming the worst:

- "I've seen a black umbrella before and that was fine – but that yellow umbrella over there is definitely going to eat me."
- "I've never heard that noise before – it must mean the end of the world."
- "Mum/Dad dropped his/her shoulders in training – I'm going to go off and sniff to console myself."
- "New venue equals no way!"
- "I got it wrong, there's just no chance I can get it right!"

These are just a few examples. Pessimism taints every interaction, learning opportunity and choice your dog makes. Revisiting that warren of choice tunnels: pessimism blocks half of them. That eliminates 50 per cent of the available choices – and, generally, those are the choices you want your dog to make!

Optimism-Pessimism are inherent characteristics of us humans too, and, while not the remit of this section, they can also affect our dog training.

Human Optimism-Pessimism Test

"The doctor measured Fido's growth." What do you understand from this statement?

Did you read it as:

- Measuring how tall Fido had grown.
- Assessing how overweight he was?
- Worse still, measuring the 'growth' on his back?

Characteristics of optimism and pessimism in dogs (and many other species) have received attention in research, and a standardised test has been created, and specifically tested, in relation to dogs suffering with separation anxiety. The study demonstrated that there was a significant difference in a measure of optimism and pessimism ('judgement bias') between individuals without separation anxiety and those with. Those with separation anxiety judged new or strange things more negatively (Mendl et al., 2010).

Dog Optimism-Pessimism Test

A bowl is placed in one of two locations in either corner of a room:

- When the bowl is in one location (positive), there is always a piece of cheese in it.
- When the bowl is in the opposite location (negative), there is never a piece of cheese in it.
- The dog is kept behind a screen (4 metres away in the standardised test) and released to the bowl

- As the outcome of approaching the bowl changes depending on its location – sometimes results in eating cheese and sometimes not – the dog learns it is not worth going to the non-rewarded side or, if he does go, he will move very slowly.
- Once the dog has learnt this discrimination, the bowl is placed in positions between the two sides.
- At the extreme, the very pessimistic dog would not approach the bowl, even if it deviated slightly from the reward side. At the other extreme, the very optimistic dog presumed there would be cheese in the bowl, even though it was extremely close to the non-rewarded position.

INDICATORS OF OPTIMISM/PESSIMISM

event	optimist	pessimist
Presented with an **unusual object** in the middle of the room	May not change behaviour and carry on or may assess object and then move on	May show avoidance of object, change behaviour or implement a coping strategy, e.g. sniffing the ground
A **usual object** has moved place in the room (e.g. a lamp or chair in the living room)	May not change behaviour and carry on or may assess object and then move on	May show avoidance of object, change behaviour or implement a coping strategy, e.g. sniffing the ground

event	optimist	pessimist
During a training session, your dog offers a behaviour in response to a cue or in a shaping session and **you** remain completely still and unresponsive **(ambiguous)** for a few seconds	May try the same thing again or may try something new	May leave you or may implement a coping strategy like sniffing, itching, etc. May struggle to try again
A **dog** freezes or gives another **ambiguous** signal	May move on or try an alternative behaviour	May become worried and react
A person behaves, is dressed or adopts a posture or outline that is **unusual**	May not change behaviour and carry on or may assess them and then move on.	May become worried and react

If you observe your dog's day-to-day behaviour you will be able to gauge his outlook on life. Adapted from Mendl et al., 2010

REACTIVITY FOCUS

When I am taking a consultation, a thorough history will often reveal that a dog who appears to have a very specific problem (for example, reacting to other dogs, reacting to people, separation anxiety, reacting to noises), is guided by his pessimistic nature.

A pessimistic outlook leads to many events, whether new, ambiguous or slightly strange, being perceived as being scary. Returning to the analogy of the bucket, this leads to the bucket being mostly full, all the time, because the dog reacts pessimistically to a wide range of small triggers. So much so,

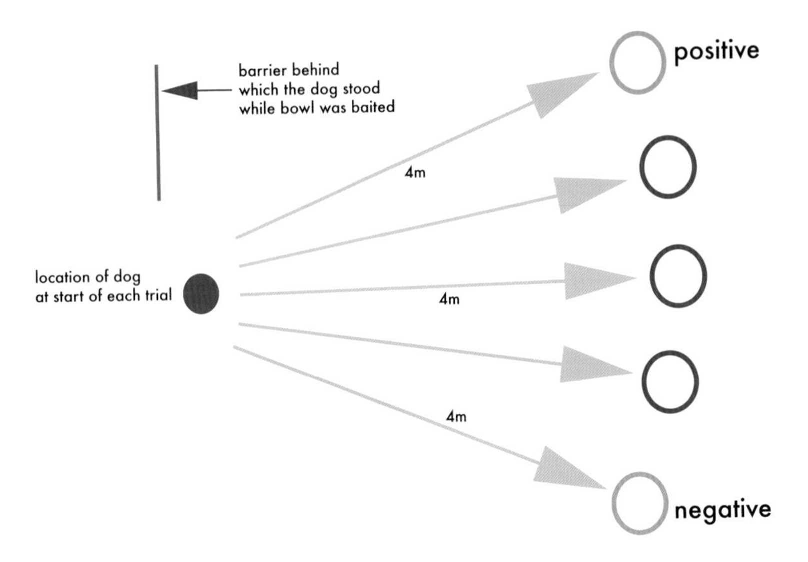

Work out whether your dog is an optimist or a pessimist – or somewhere in-between…

the presenting problem is often the tip of the iceberg. The triggers that are commonly and specifically occurring, cause the dog to go over threshold, and all that has come before it can often be missed.

This is a really important distinction to make, and can determine success or failure when working with a reactive dog. The approach to resolving the problem is determined by whether the dog is reacting to something specific, or whether the reactivity is completely, or in part, governed by an underlying pessimism. Trying to work with a reactive dog when he has a constantly full bucket, due to general pessimism, is next to impossible. On the flip side, forgetting the specific presenting problem (for example dog reactivity) and working solely on building optimism might improve, or eventually resolve, his reactivity. You will be creating an emptier bucket, further from threshold, and therefore less likely to go over threshold.

OPTIMIST VERSUS PESSIMIST

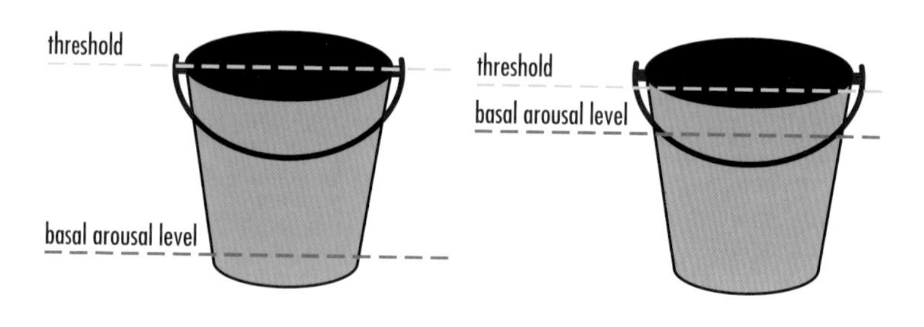

The basal arousal level of the optimist is well below the threshold which maximises his ability to process what is going on and to pick the 'right' behaviour.

GAMES TO PLAY

Building optimism could not be more rewarding – and it is so much fun! There are a number of games that will help your dog to become an optimist:

Shaping

This involves rewarding approximations of a behaviour until you arrive at what you want. When you shape, you are driving choices towards an end goal by rewarding the choices that are heading in the right direction.

For example, this is how I shape a duration down with a release on a bed:

- Reward your dog for looking at the mat.
- Reward him for stepping towards the mat.
- Reward him for stepping on to the mat.
- Reward two feet on the mat.
- Reward three/four feet on the mat, and place reward low to the ground.

- Reward a weight shift back while he is on the mat and place reward low.
- Reward a weight shift back that leads to his rear hitting ground while he is on the mat, and place reward low.
- Reward duration.
- Reward duration, say release cue ("free", "release" or "break") and throw the reward away from the mat to promote moving off.

Shaping is an amazing optimism builder because it communicates to your dog that, when he is presented with uncertainty, ambiguity or a new situation, trying something results in a positive outcome (food!).

Specific shaping exercises that I really like for building optimism include:

Shaping a nose target into a muzzle: This is a vital skill to train but it is also very useful in building optimism. After all, if you can shape your dog to put his muzzle into a cone or similar shaped object, thereby cutting off some of his senses, he must be feeling pretty optimistic to do so!

Shaping wrapping around a pole: This is a great starter in shaping for many dogs. It involves a lot of movement, which helps dogs that lack confidence, and it is a great one for taking on the road and reshaping (see Reshaping, page 191).

Shaping front feet on an object/Back feet on an object/ Walking under an object/Walking over an object: These are great optimism and confidence builders – and build flexibility in the learner, too!

Shaping with the Environment

Shaping with the environment is great for dogs that lack optimism out and about. The behaviour you are shaping is irrelevant; I would say that 90 per cent of the shaping I do with my dogs, and other people's dogs, is without a final purpose.

The aim is to build and develop specific concepts which will enhance their personality.

Behaviours to shape with the environment out and about might be:

- Wrapping a tree.
- Placing back feet on a tree stump.
- Placing four feet in a shopping basket on the floor.
- Reversing up steps.
- Ducking under branches or bars.
- Jumping over logs.

Reshaping

This is something I have already discussed in relation to generalising (see page 91). It's a game I employ when:

- I need to build the skill of generalisation, whether that is a companion dog that needs consistency between environments or a sports dog that struggles to transfer learning to competition, for example.
- I need to build thought and learning ability in an exciting/arousing environment.
- I need to build optimism, especially in reactivity behaviour cases, or in dogs whose speed or intensity is environmentally sensitive.

Reshaping is a term I invented; it simply means starting from scratch shaping something that your dog already knows. For example, you may train your dog to place four feet in a box in the home environment. You would then go to a new environment and start from scratch, shaping the behaviour all over again.

The choices (tunnels) your dog will pick have already been primed and enhanced to make the decisions easier, more instant, and therefore made with more confidence. Each time

you reward your dog for making the right choice, placing one foot in the box, for example, you are boosting his confidence and enhancing the pathway even more!

It is an especially powerful game to play with pessimists or simply as a means of building confidence. It communicates that moments of uncertainty are followed by positive outcomes. Even more importantly for the sports dog, it shows that trying things and experimenting – despite the uncertainty – brings success! This makes the game especially useful for dogs (or owners) that have a fear of failure in training sessions.

Distraction, Mark, Treat!

This game has a range of applications. I use it for:

- Lack of focus.
- General over-arousal problems.
- Over-arousal in training and competition settings.
- General anxiety problems.
- Specific fear responses.
- Multiple fear responses.
- Developing an optimist.

The aim of this protocol is to reduce arousal (excitement) in the face of distractions, and to create and maintain a positive emotional response with these events. In the case of building an optimist, this is developing a calm and positive emotional response to all new events as they occur, and to all ambiguous situations. In terms of working with over-arousal, you need to bear in mind that each distraction and element of the environment can increase arousal a little. In a challenging environment, for example in competition or training environments, arousal can increase dramatically, leading to over-arousal or reactivity.

DISTRACTION, MARK, TREAT

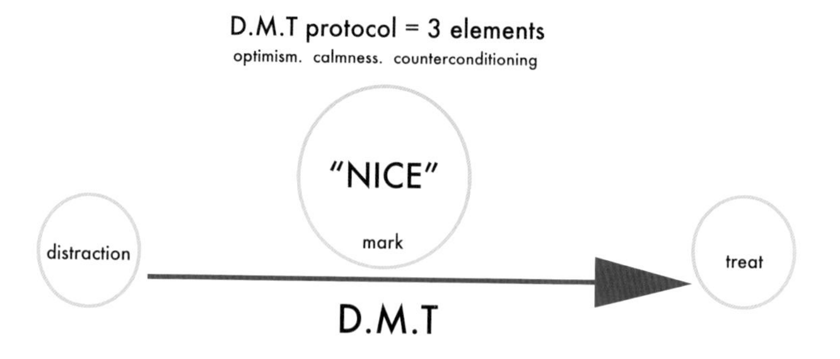

When faced with a distraction, the marker word is followed by a tasty treat.

This game involves three elements:

1. **Distraction:** This could be any event in the environment – for example, a person appearing in the distance, a leaf falling from a tree, a dog barking in house next door.
2. **Mark:** A marker is a word or sound that signals to your dog that a treat (or positive event) is on the way. In this protocol, I recommend the word "nice", spoken in a calm and soft voice.
3. **Treat:** Your dog's food will be used in this protocol. When the distraction in question occurs (e.g. dog barks in distance, dog appears on horizon), you will mark the event as something positive ("nice") and follow with the treat. It's that simple!

In the case of building an optimist, this can and should be anything and everything new that occurs in an environment. In this context, 'new' does not necessarily mean something your dog has never encountered before – but rather something that is new to the current situation.

BUILDING OPTIMISM

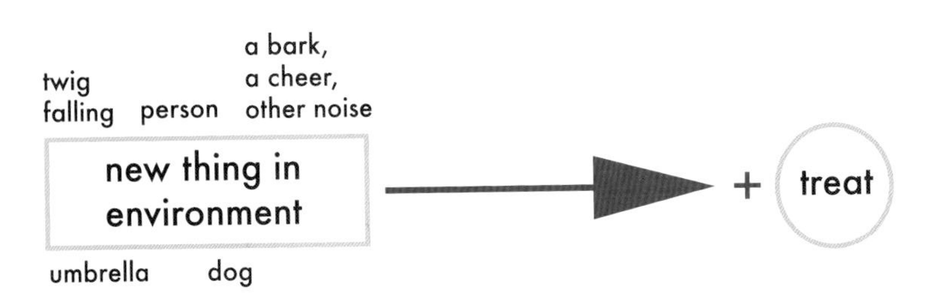

Everything new should be marked and treated, so your dog embraces change.

Investing in optimism and boosting that optimism bank account is the most amazing gift you could give to any dog. With companion dogs, you unlock real confidence and happiness in their environments. With sports dogs, you unlock that next level of learning and performance. Finally, and possibly most importantly, with Naughty but Nice dogs, you move to a world of preparing them for every event that hasn't even happened yet, becoming proactive in their scary worlds rather than adopting the same reactive approach that they themselves all too often adopt. Optimism is powerful.

Mendl, M., Brooks, J., Basse, C., Burman, O., Paul, E., Blackwell, E. & Casey, R. 2010a, Dogs showing separation-related behaviour exhibit a "pessimistic" cognitive bias, *Current Biology*, 20, R839–R840.

SECTION III: MOVEMENT

CHAPTER 17 THE CONCEPT OF MOVEMENT

Movement is rarely considered as a concept in its own right, yet it has the most wide-ranging application. Regardless of the role we select – companion dog, obedience or agility competitor, gundog or police dog – our dogs will spend a large proportion of their time moving. With every type of movement, there is a form and style that is the most efficient, effective and safe.

TYPES OF MOVEMENT

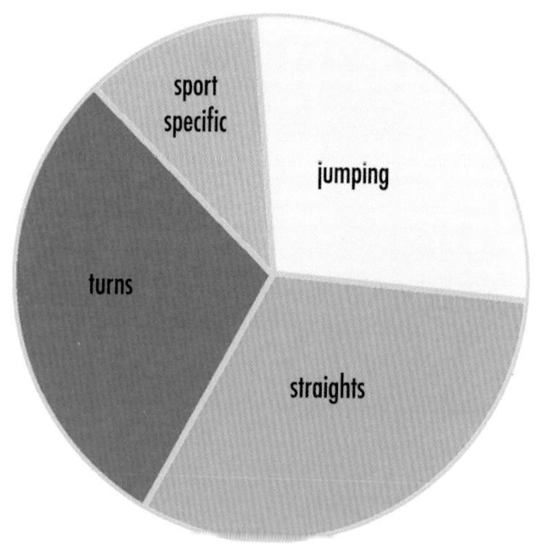

Each type of movement demands a specific skill set.

Movement differs from the other concepts we have considered because a weakness in this skill area can lead directly to injury. Poor movement can lead to abnormal loading of joints and repetition of small, cumulative trauma to musculoskeletal tissues.

Abnormal movement patterns, whether that be in simpler but more often used movements, such as walking, or higher order movements that are more complex, such as jumping, can have profound implications in terms of injury and longevity of pain-free performance. Regardless of whether the movement relates to their daily lives or to their sports and jobs, our dogs are moving all the time, which is why abnormal movement patterns are so crucial.

Three overarching movement types are consistent among all lifestyles and all sports:

- Straights (walking, trotting and flat-out running).
- Turns.
- Jumps.

In addition, there are a number of sport-specific movement types that, while beyond the remit of this book, are equally important in developing the correct form of movement for success in their respective sports. Examples of such may be heelwork for the obedience competitor, weaving for the agility competitor, or bouncing off the board for the flyball competitor – efficient, effective and safe movement to carry out these specialist skills is crucial.

An understanding of the skills your dog needs, coupled with an understanding of his own unique structure is key. This often requires input from a variety of professionals who will be able to assess your dog's conformation, lifestyle and current movement, and advise accordingly.

The starting point is an awareness that movement must suit the job in hand, which, along with structure, impacts on all the behaviours a dog is taught throughout his life. This applies equally, regardless of whether you are aiming for an injury-free

and stress-free game of retrieve with your companion dog, or whether you are aspiring to win in the agility ring.

Now, a confession: movement isn't really a concept like the others. It doesn't taint the way a dog approaches a situation, the choices he makes, or his emotional responses. Movement types are simply different behaviours (think choice of tunnels, all over again). But these elementary behaviours are so far-reaching, so intertwined with future learning, and with such implications on health and wellbeing (partly due to a large involvement of firing at the spinal cord level as well as in the brain), it seems only right to give them due attention.

This is made easier because movement obeys the same rules as other behaviours: we can promote what we like, reward and rehearse efficient, effective and safe movement such that our dogs will repeat and perform them as needed now and in the future.

ENHANCING MOVEMENT

game	movement type	movement criteria to reward	things not to reward
Race to Dead Toy Restrain your dog ahead of a toy on the ground, release him and race him to it. If he moves incorrectly, e.g. pounces or stalks, beat him to the toy. If he moves especially well, e.g. with low head carriage, then let him win the race!	**Flat-Out Running Straights**	Low head Flat out running Effective acceleration Forward focus and commitment Independence of you	Pouncing Bouncing Flanking (curving as seen in herding, especially in certain breeds) Eye stalk
Race to Food Bowl Place a bowl with kibble on the ground. Move some distance away, and restrain your dog so he is directly in front of the food bowl. Release him and race him to it. If he moves in a way that you don't like, beat him to the bowl. If he moves especially well, then let him get there first and have a party	**Flat-Out Running Straights**	Low head Flat out running Effective acceleration Forward focus and commitment Independence	Pouncing Bouncing Flanking (curving as seen in herding, especially in certain breeds) Eye stalk

game	movement type	movement criteria to reward	things not to reward
Whip-It Game Get your dog to chase a toy on the end of a lunge whip. Animate the toy as if it is alive Reward different aspects of the movement by letting him get the toy when he moves in that way. Bad movement leads to him losing his prey	**Flat-Out Running Straights**	Low head No bounciness Effective acceleration Forward Focus and commitment Independence Tight turns Effective running in arousal	Pouncing Bouncing Eye stalk
Restrained Recalls Ask someone to restrain your dog, run ahead and recall him and reward in your hand! If he flanks, runs past you or becomes bouncy, withhold the reward	**Flat-Out Running Straights**	Low Head Effective acceleration Effective deceleration (lack of overshooting) Effective running in arousal	Bouncing Flanking Overshooting
Flat-Out Racing with Other Dogs Get together with other friendly dogs and send them to race one another in a safe place. This game doesn't involve rewarding good aspects of the movement but dogs usually show very effective movement when racing other dogs so is a great opportunity to release the good stuff	**Flat-Out Running Straights**	Low Head Effective acceleration Effective deceleration No bounciness Forward focus and commitment Effective running in arousal	N/A
Cavaletti Place some jump poles on the ground and ask your dog to walk over them. There are some really cool set-ups to do but generally, in healthy dogs, as long as you don't overdo any one set-up, then you can't go wrong. **Natural Cavaletti** is just that – nature! Take your dog to the woods and have fun!	**Flat-Out Running Straights**	Limb Awareness	Tripping or knocking poles Bouncing Stepping over multiple poles

game	movement type	movement criteria to reward	things not to reward
Grids A grid is a set-up of a series of jumps, often on varying heights. These are developed to train jump style.	**Jumps**	Jumping in extension Effective launching Effective landing Effective anticipation and preparation Jump style in arousal Bascule-shape jumping. The bascule is the round shape to the body that a dog (or horse) should adopt in tackling a jump. And so much more!	Knocking bars Early take off Untidy style High head carriage And so on…

We can harness the powers of rehearsal and reinforcement strategy and create optimum movement form. In the case of movement, the most important and powerful of these two learning techniques is rehearsal.

This is, in part, because a lot of movement is signalled at the level of the spinal cord, without the involvement of the brain. Therefore, just as bad movement patterns can become rehearsed and ingrained, we can flip this and instead ensure rehearsal of the good stuff. To better our dogs' movement, we must limit rehearsal of the abnormal movement pattern while rehearsing the desired movement pattern. Just as with every concept, games are fundamental to achieving this.

ADVANCED GAIT WORK FOR FITNESS

An incredibly valuable exercise for building core strength and developing movement skills is to rehearse transitioning between gaits in a straight line. Gait is the pattern with which limbs hit the ground when moving in a straight line – for example, when walking or trotting.

When a dog walks, each limb hits the ground individually. This four-step movement is called a four-beat gait pattern. The trot, however, is a two-beat gait pattern with diagonal opposite

limbs moving in unison. There are other gait patterns, but I focus on walking and trotting in this type of advanced work. Developing and rehearsing these gaits with your dog is a great conditioning exercise in itself.

Some of the dogs I come across in my work as a trainer and as a vet struggle with gait and, quite simply, have never had the opportunity to rehearse it. Typically, dogs struggle with the walk, insisting on going everywhere at speed. These dogs often struggle with being calm in the household as they inevitably end up in a cycle of not walking, leading to increased arousal, leading to even more difficulty in trying to walk. The situation does not improve until a low basal level of arousal is established (calmness) and walking is practised. Rehearsal of the individual gaits is the first step in this type of training.

The second step is to assess transitions between gaits. These transitions require a lot of strength, especially of the core musculature, but equally require fine-tuned neurological control. With your dog on lead, start in a walk and then increase speed to a trot. How will you know if your dog struggles with the transition? Well, typically, if he struggles, he will bounce, loose-lead walking will be erratic, he will lose focus, and his back legs may skip or they may miss a beat. The key is practice, making sure to reward the movement you like.

Now, see if your dog can switch down in gait patterns, from trotting to walking. This type of low impact muscular and neurological conditioning exercise builds the concept of effective movement, and it is easy to do as it can be incorporated into your daily walks.

PROTECTING MOVEMENT

When your dog is lame (limping) or has any kind of soreness, whether that relates to a limb, illness (e.g. gastrointestinal disease) or a surgical procedure, movement will be affected. This may be in the form of walking with a limp, or it may be walking hunched. In both cases – based on the principles

outlined above – we need to ensure limited rehearsal of bad movement patterns.

An example of this is the dogs I see that have just been neutered. These dogs typically walk with a slight hunch to their topline; they resent extending their hind-limbs, wanting to avoid applying tension to the internal and external wounds, and they are often sore but cope with the soreness by appearing hyperactive and a little crazy.

The temptation, here, would be to get them walking and burning energy, in a safe manner, soon after surgery. Whereas, it would be more appropriate to limit rehearsal of the bad movement patterns (highlighted above) to avoid lasting abnormalities. In addition, we should manage their pain better and employ them in some calm activities that are not movement-based.

Most vets advise restricted exercise following neutering (or other abdominal surgery) for at least two weeks based on the rough healing time of wounds. In actual fact, this may be the best thing to do for different reasons.

The same principles apply to misused equipment, for example an ill-fitting harness or head collar, or allowing a dog to pull on a collar. These develop and rehearse abnormal movement patterns.

Movement is powerful – it taints and influences everything we do with our dogs. However, it is completely in our control to influence this powerful force, so we can make our dogs resilient to injury and increase their pain-free existence, too. If that wasn't enough, training movement as a concept can create super talented sports dogs, promote fit and healthy dogs, and ensure success.

IN SUMMARY

Concepts are powerful; by becoming a concept trainer, coupled with a good understanding of dog learning and flexible and situation-specific reinforcement strategy (all discussed in this book), you truly can achieve success in any field. Whether you currently are dealing with training issues with your companion dog, sports dog or naughty but nice dog, becoming a concept trainer turns struggles into strengths.

If you need:

- To build ***flexibility*** so your dog can tackle situations differently.
- To develop ***focus*** as a concept such that it transfers everywhere and anywhere.
- More ability to ***think in arousal*** so that your dog's learning is not sensitive to the exciting (and scary) world we live in.
- Awesome ***optimism*** so that everything new equals a good thing.
- To enhance ***calmness*** and ability to ***switch up and down*** in arousal.
- Increased ability to ***generalise*** such that the same learning can be applied to different situations.
- To harness the power of ***true grit*** for a super little worker.
- A ***thinker*** or a ***doer*** or both.

- Super ***tolerance of frustration*** to prepare for an unpredictable and changing world.

...always remember that playing games teaches concepts.

Concepts create your dog's personality, and it is with this personality that he approaches each and every situation in his life. If you become a concept trainer, you have the ability to change and manipulate your dog's mindset so that he

MEL TAYLOR PHOTOGRAPHY

By embracing the world of concept training, you will get the very best from your dog – and enjoy a rich and rewarding relationship with him.

can achieve his full potential, whether that is being a well-balanced companion dog or a star performer in the agility ring. Concept training allows you to resolve the most complex and scary problems simply by playing fun games that appear to be completely detached from the problem situation. Equally, concept training can be used shape your dog's thinking so that it acts as a preventative, develops his skills and helps you to achieve success – simply by playing games.

The key to making this happen is to identify the concepts that are needed to overcome a struggle or to achieving a dream. The hardest bit of concept training is determining which concepts are involved in the struggle, and what would benefit from being improved. Once you identify the concepts needed, the games are a cinch. Whether you are a professional trainer, a behaviourist or instructor, or whether you just want to achieve your dog-human team's potential, concept training is key.

It becomes a simple three step process:

- **Firstly**, you have to decide what struggle or dream you want to tackle.
- **Next**, sit down and think which of the concepts are needed to achieve what you want.
- **Finally**, check which games build the concepts and start playing!

Personality is fluid and, using concept training, you can enhance, develop and strengthen behavioural traits that suit your dog, his job and you. This will inevitably require lots of revisiting throughout your dog's life but now you have the tools to consider concepts and build them. Play games, teach concepts and get success – whatever that means to you!